Piano · Vocal · Guitar

THE ESSENTIAL JOHNNY CASH

Cover photo appears courtesy of the Country Music Hall of Fame.

Interior photos appear courtesy of Johnny Cash's personal collection.

ISBN 0-7935-7583-4

HAL•LEONARD®
CORPORATION

7777 W. BLUEMOUND RD. P.O. BOX 13819 MILWAUKEE, WI 53213

Visit Hal Leonard Online at
www.halleonard.com

CONTENTS

SELECTED ALBUM DISCOGRAPHY

THE FABULOUS JOHNNY CASH
(Columbia) 1958
Don't Take Your Guns to Town; Frankie's Man, Johnny; I Still Miss Someone; I'd Rather Die Young; One More Ride; Pickin' Time; Run Softly; Blue River; Shepherd of My Heart; Supper-Time; That's All Over; That's Enough; The Troubador

BLOOD, SWEAT & TEARS (Columbia) 1963
Another Man Done Gone; Busted; Casey Jones; Chain Gang; Legend of John Henry's Hammer; Nine Pound Hammer; Roughneck; Tell Him I'm Gone; Waiting for a Train

RING OF FIRE (THE BEST OF JOHNNY CASH)
(Columbia) 1963
The Big Battle; Bonanza!; Forty Shades of Green; I Still Miss Someone; I'd Still Be There; The Rebel-Johnny Yuma; Remember the Alamo; Ring of Fire; Tennessee Flat Top Box; (There'll Be) Peace in the Valley (For Me); Were You There (When They Crucified My Lord); What Do I Care

I WALK THE LINE (Columbia) 1964
Bad News; Big River; Folsom Prison Blues; Give My Love to Rose; Goodbye, Little Darlin' Goodbye; Hey Porter; I Still Miss Someone; I Walk the Line; Still in Town; Troublesome Waters; Understand Your Man; Wreck of the Old 97

BITTER TEARS
(BALLADS OF THE AMERICAN INDIAN)
(Columbia) 1964
Apache Tears; As Long as the Grass Shall Grow; Ballad of Ira Hayes; Custer; Drums; Talking Leaves; Vanishing Race; White Girl

ORANGE BLOSSOM SPECIAL (Columbia) 1965
All of God's Children Ain't Free; Amen; Danny Boy; Don't Think Twice, It's All Right; It Ain't Me, Babe; Long Black Veil; Mama, You Been on My Mind; Orange Blossom Special; The Wall; When It's Springtime in Alaska (It's Forty Below); Wildwood Flower; You Wild Colorado

EVERYBODY LOVES A NUT (Columbia) 1966
Austin Prison; Boa Constrictor; Bug That Tried to Crawl Around the World; Cup of Coffee; Dirty Old Egg-Sucking Dog; Everybody Loves a Nut; Joe Bean; One on the Right Is on the Left; Please Don't Play Red River Valley; Singing Star's Queen; Take Me Home

JOHNNY CASH'S GREATEST HITS; VOLUME 1
(Columbia) 1967
Ballad of Ira Hayes; Don't Take Your Guns to Town; Five Feet High and Rising; I Walk the Line; It Ain't Me, Babe; Jackson; One on the Right Is on the Left; Orange Blossom Special; The Rebel-Johnny Yuma; Ring of Fire; Understand Your Man

CARRYIN' ON WITH JOHNNY CASH AND JUNE CARTER (Columbia) 1967
Fast Boat to Sydney; I Got a Woman; It Ain't Me, Babe; Jackson; Long-Legged Guitar Pickin' Man; No, No, No; Oh, What a Good Thing We Had; Pack Up Your Sorrows; Shantytown; What'd I Say; You'll Be All Right

JOHNNY CASH AT FOLSOM PRISON
(Columbia) 1968
Cocaine Blues; Dark as a Dungeon; Dirty Old Egg-Sucking Dog; Flushed from the Bathroom of Your Heart; Folsom Prison Blues; Give My Love to Rose; Green, Green Grass of Home; Greystone Chapel; I Got Stripes; I Still Miss Someone; Jackson; Long Black Veil; Orange Blossom Special; Send a Picture of Mother; 25 Minutes to Go; The Wall

THE HOLY LAND (Columbia) 1969
At Calvary; At the Wailing Wall; Beautiful Words; Church of the Holy Sepulchre; Come to the Wailing Wall; Daddy Sang Bass; Fourth Man; God Is Not Dead; Guess Things Happen That Way; He Turned the Water into Wine; In Bethlehem; In Garden of Gethsemane; Land of Israel; Mother's Love; My Wife June at Sea of Galilee; Nazarene; On the Via Dolorosa; Our Guide Jacob at Mount Tabor; Ten Commandments; This Is Nazareth; Town of Cana

JOHNNY CASH AT SAN QUENTIN
(Columbia) 1969
A Boy Named Sue; Darling Companion; Folsom Prison Blues; I Walk the Line; San Quentin; Starkville City Jail; (There'll Be) Peace in the Valley (For Me); Wanted Man; Wreck of the Old 97

ORIGINAL GOLDEN HITS; VOLUME I (Sun) 1969
Cry, Cry, Cry; Don't Make Me Go; Folsom Prison Blues; Get Rhythm; Hey Porter; Home of the Blues; I Walk the Line; Next in Line; So Doggone Lonesome; There You Go; Train of Love

ORIGINAL GOLDEN HITS; VOLUME II (Sun) 1969
Ballad of a Teenage Queen; Big River; Come in, Stranger; Give My Love to Rose; Guess Things Happen That Way; I Just Thought You'd Like to Know; Just About Time; Luther's Boogie; Thanks a Lot; Ways of a Woman in Love; You're the Nearest Thing to Heaven

JOHNNY CASH (Harmony) 1969
Bad News; Don't Think Twice, It's All Right; Frankie's Man, Johnny; I Still Miss Someone; Long Black Veil; Lorena; Nine Pound Hammer; Streets of Loredo; When Papa Played the Dobro

GET RHYTHM (Sun) 1969
Belshazah; Country Boy; Doin' My Time; Get Rhythm; Luther's Boogie; Mean Eyed Cat; New Mexico; Oh Lonesome Me; Sugartime; Two Timin' Woman; You Win Again

SHOWTIME (Sun) 1969
Ballad of a Teenage Queen; Big River; Come in, Stranger; Cry, Cry, Cry; Folsom Prison Blues; Guess Things Happen That Way; Hey Porter; I Walk the Line; Rock Island Line; There You Go; Wreck of the Old 97

STORY SONGS OF THE TRAINS AND RIVERS
(Sun) 1969
Big River; Blue Train; Down the Street to 301; Hey Porter; I Heard That Lonesome Whistle; Life Goes On; Port of Lonely Hearts; Rock Island Line; Train of Love; Wide Open Road; Wreck of the Old 97

HELLO, I'M JOHNNY CASH (Columbia) 1970
Blistered; 'Cause I Love You; Devil to Pay; I've Got a Thing About Trains; If I Were a Carpenter; Jesus Was a Carpenter; Route #1, Box 144; See Ruby Fall; Sing a Traveling Song; Southwind; To Beat the Devil; Wrinkled, Crinkled, Wadded Dollar Bill

THE SINGING STORYTELLER (Sun) 1970
Come in, Stranger; Give My Love to Rose; Goodbye, Little Darlin' Goodbye; Hey Good Lookin'; I Can't Help It; I Could Never Be Ashamed of You; I Couldn't Keep from Crying; I Love You Because; Next in Line; Ways of a Woman in Love; You're the Nearest Thing to Heaven

THE WORLD OF JOHNNY CASH
(Columbia) 1970
Accidentally on Purpose; Busted; Casey Jones; Delia's Gone; Frankie's Man, Johnny; I Feel Better All Over; I Forgot More than You'll Ever Know; I Still Miss Someone; I Want to Go Home; I'm So Lonesome I Could Cry; In the Jailhouse Now; In Them Old Cottonfields Back Home; Legend of John Henry's Hammer; My Shoes Keep Walking Back to You; One More Ride; Pickin' Time; Sing It Pretty, Sue; Supper-Time; Waiting for a Train; When Papa Played the Dobro

THE JOHNNY CASH SHOW (Columbia) 1970
Come Along and Ride This Train Medley I & II; Here Was a Man; I'm Gonna Try to Be That Way; Sunday Mornin' Comin' Down; These Hands

I WALK THE LINE (Columbia) 1970
Amazing Grace (Medley); 'Cause I Love You; Face of Despair; Flesh and Blood; Hungry; I Walk the Line; Standing on the Promises (Medley); This Side of the Law; This Town; World's Gonna Fall on You

MAN IN BLACK (Columbia) 1971
Dear Mrs.; I Talk to Jesus Every Day; If Not for Love; Look for Me; The Man in Black; Ned Kelly; Orphan of the Road; Preacher Said, "Jesus Said"; Singin' in Viet Nam Talkin' Blues; You've Got a New Light Shining in Your Eyes

THE JOHNNY CASH COLLECTION
(HIS GREATEST HITS; VOLUME II)
(Columbia) 1971
Big River; Blistered; A Boy Named Sue; Daddy Sang Bass; Folsom Prison Blues; Frankie's Man, Johnny; Guess Things Happen That Way; Hey Porter; If I Were a Carpenter; Long-Legged Guitar Pickin' Man; Sunday Morning Coming Down

A THING CALLED LOVE (Columbia) 1972
Arkansas Lovin' Man; Daddy; I Promise You, Kate; Melva's Wine; Miracle Man; Mississippi Sand; Papa Was a Good Man; Tear Stained Letter; Thing Called Love

JOHNNY CASH: AMERICA
(A 200-YEAR SALUTE IN STORY AND SONG)
(Columbia) 1972

Battle of New Orleans; Begin West Movement;
Big Battle; Big Foot; Come Take a Trip in My
Airship; Gettysburg Address; Like a Young Colt;
Lorena; Mister Garfield; On Wheels and Wings;
Opening the West; Paul Revere; Proud Land;
Reaching for the Stars; Remember the Alamo;
Road to Kaintuck; Southwestward; These Are My
People; To the Shining Mountains; The West

ANY OLD WIND THAT BLOWS (Columbia) 1973
Any Old Wind That Blows; Ballad of Annie Palmer;
Best Friend; Country Trash; Good Earth; If I Had a
Hammer; Kentucky Straight; Loving Gift; Oney;
Too Little, Too Late; Welcome Back Jesus

ONE PIECE AT A TIME (Columbia) 1976
Committed to Parkview; Daughter of a Railroad
Man; Go On Blues; In a Young Girl's Mind; Let
There Be Country; Love Has Lost Again; Michigan
City Howdy Do; Mountain Lady; One Piece at a
Time; Sold Out of Flagpoles

HIGHWAYMAN (Columbia) 1985
Against the Wind; Big River; Committed to
Parkview; Deportee (Plane Wreck at Los Gatos);
Desperados Waiting for a Train; Highwayman;
Jim, I Wore a Tie Today; Last Cowboy Song;
Twentieth Century Is Almost Over; Welfare Line

CLASS OF '55
(MEMPHIS ROCK AND ROLL HOMECOMING)
(Columbia) 1986

Big Train (From Memphis); Birth of Rock and Roll;
Class of '55; Coming Home; I Will Rock and Roll
with You; Keep My Motor Running; Rock and Roll
(Fais-Do-Do); Sixteen Candles; Waymore's Blues;
We Remember the King

HIGHWAYMAN 2 (Columbia) 1990
American Remains; Angels Love Bad Men;
Anthem '84; Born and Raised in Black and White;
Living Legend; Silver Stallion; Songs That Make a
Difference; Texas; Two Stories Wide; We're All in
Your Corner

AMERICAN RECORDINGS (American) 1994
Beast in Me; Bird on a Wire; Delia's Gone; Down
There by the Train; Drive On; Let the Train Blow
the Whistle; Like a Soldier; Man Who Couldn't
Cry; Oh Bury Me Not; Redemption; Tennessee
Stud; Thirteen; Why Me Lord

AFTER THE BALL

Words and Music by
JOHN R. CASH

I hear peo - ple laugh - in' on the cor -
Lov - in' you is sweet ad - dic - tion,

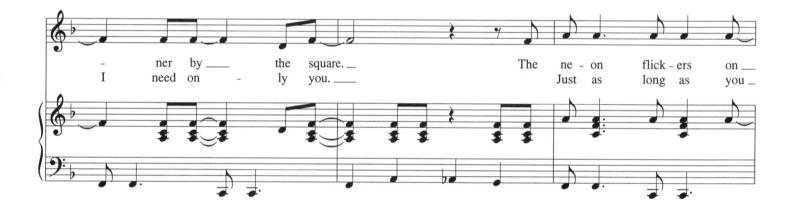

- ner by ___ the square. ___ The ne - on flick - ers on ___
I need on - ly you. ___ Just as long as you ___

___ my wall ___ and I ___ know you're out there. ___ I'm in your bed and
come back, ___ oh, do ___ what you want to. ___ Give the night your

lis-ten-in' for your foot-steps down the hall. ___
laugh-ter, but I'll have you af-ter all. ___ } And I'll ___ be

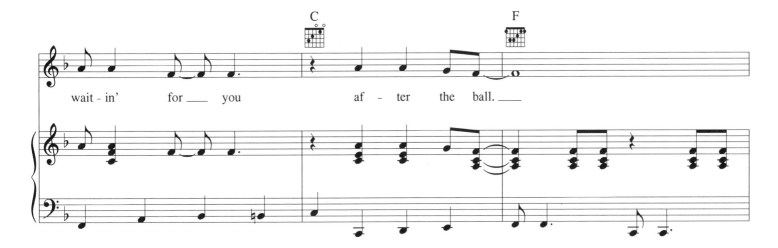

wait-in' for ___ you af-ter the ball. ___

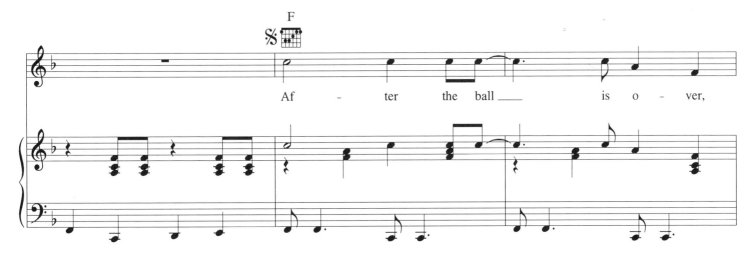

Af - ter the ball ___ is o - ver,

af - ter the ball. ___ If you can-not stand, I've got a place ___

for you to fall. The blinds are drawn and I have turned the clock

face to the wall. I'll be wait-in' for you

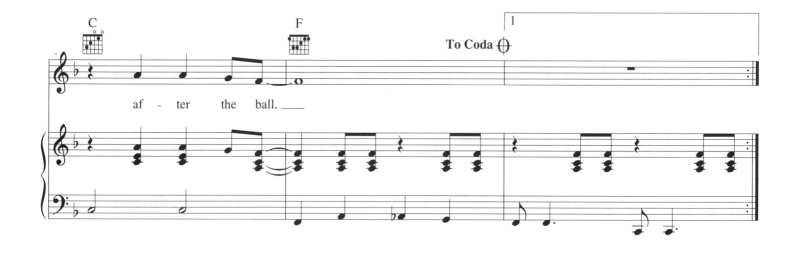

af - ter the ball.

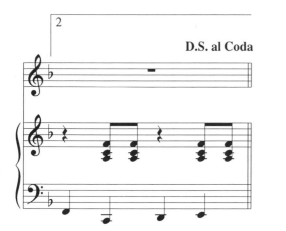

All Over Again

Words and Music by
JOHNNY R. CASH

Moderately Bright

CHORUS

C

Ev-'ry time I look at you I fall in love

C   G7   G7

All   o - ver a - gain.   Ev-'ry time I think of

G7   G7

you it all be - gins   All   o - ver a -

gain.　　　　　　　　One lit-tle dream at night and I can

dream all day.　　It on - ly takes a mem - o - ry to

thrill me.　　　　　　One lit-tle kiss from you and I just

fly a - way.　　Pour me out your love un - til you fill me.

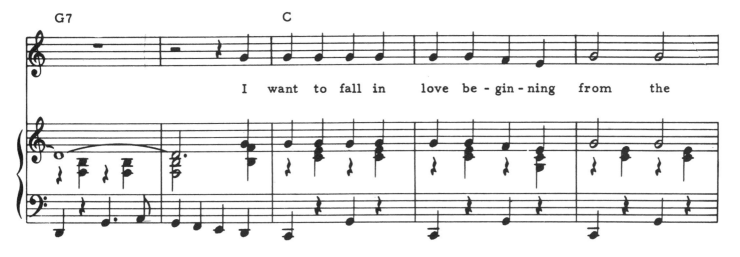

BAD NEWS

Words and Music by
JOHN D. LOUDERMILK

* Vocal line sung an octave lower than written.

bad news   ev - 'ry - where I   go. __

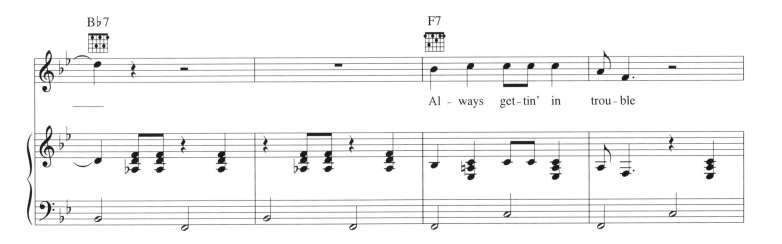

__   Al - ways get-tin' in   trou - ble

and leav-in' lit - tle girls that   hate to   see __ me   go.

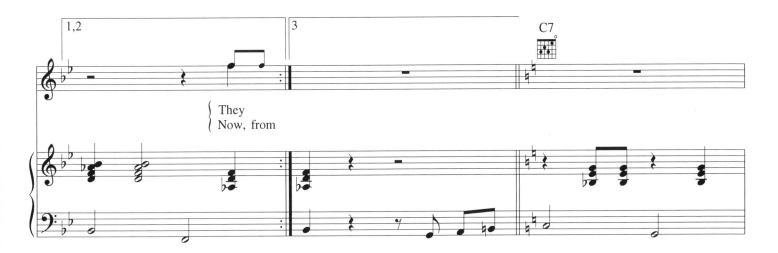

They
Now, from

ev - 'ry-where I go.

Al - ways get-tin' in - to

trou-ble and leav-in' lit-tle girls that hate to see __ me

go.

Repeat and Fade

BALLAD OF A TEENAGE QUEEN

Words and Music by
JACK CLEMENT

Additional Lyrics

4. Very soon she was a star, pretty house and shiny cars,
   Swimming pool and a fence around, but she missed her old home town.
   (But she missed her old home town)
   All the world was at her door,
   All except the boy next door, who worked at the candy store.
   Dream on, dream on, teenage queen, saddest girl we've ever seen.

5. Then one day the teenage star sold her house and all her cars.
   Gave up all her wealth and fame, left it all and caught a train.
   (Left it all and caught a train)
   Do I have to tell you more?
   She came back to the boy next door, who worked at the candy store.
   Now this story has some more; you'll hear it all at the candy store.

BALLAD OF IRA HAYES

Words and Music by
PETER LA FARGE

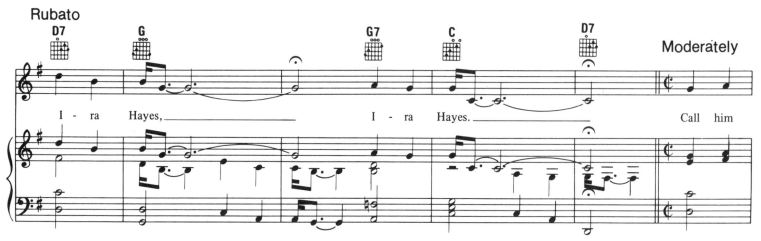

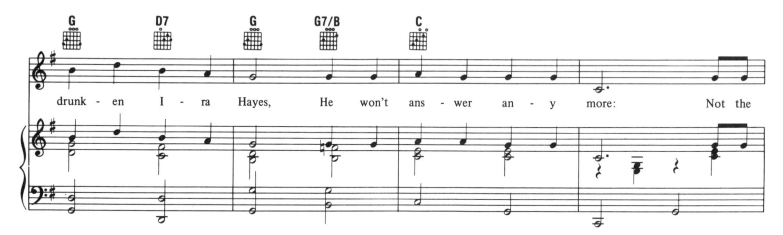

white man stole their water rights and their sparklin' water stopped. Now

Ira's folks grew hungry and their land grew crops of weeds. When

war came Ira vol - unteered and forgot the white man's greed.

Chorus

Call him drink - en I - ra Hayes, he won't

ans - wer an - y more: Not the whis - key drink - in' In - dian, Nor the ma -

rine that went to war._____

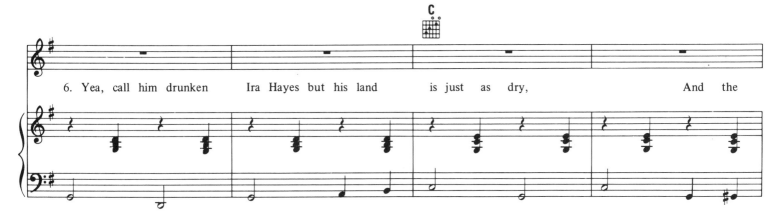

6. Yea, call him drunken Ira Hayes but his land is just as dry, And the

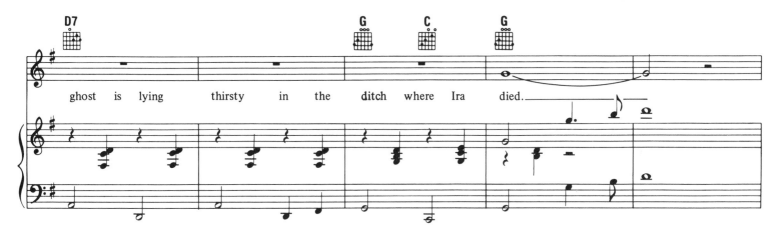

ghost is lying thirsty in the ditch where Ira died._____

rit.

3. Well, they battled up Iwo Jima Hill - two hundred and fifty men,
   But only twenty-seven lived - to walk back down again;
   When the fight was over - and Old Glory raised,
   Among the men who held it high was the Indian - Ira Hayes. (D.S.℈)

4. Ira Hayes returned a hero, - celebrated thru the land,
   He was wined and speeched and honored, - everybody shook his hand;
   But he was just a Pima Indian, - no water, no water, no home, no chance;
   At home nobody cared what Ira done - and when do the Indians dance? (D.S.℈)

5. Then Ira started drinkin' hard - jail was often his home;
   They let him raise the flag and lower it, - as you would throw a dog a bone;
   He died drunk early one morning, - alone in the land he'd fought to save;
   Two inches of water in a lonely ditch - was the grave for Ira Hayes. (D.S.℈)

Last Verse: D.S.℈al ⊕, then to Coda

THE BIG BATTLE

Words and Music by
JOHNNY R. CASH

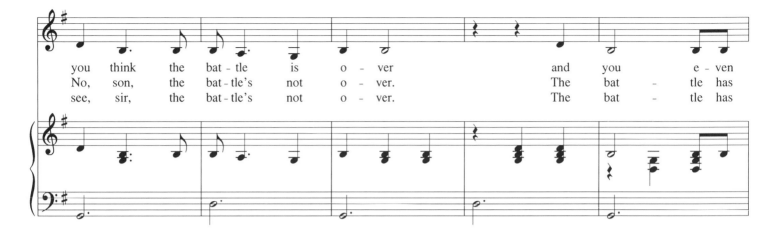

A D A
bat - tle is done. O'er sea ov - er there where we fought them
deaf - en - ing sound. For ev - 'ry shot fired had an ech - o
rest of their lives. Now qui - et - ly rise from your cov - er.
E7 A E
it's quiet for they've all gone a - way. All
and ev - 'ry man killed want - ed life.
Be thank - ful that God let you live.
A E7
left is the dead and the dy - in', the blue ly - in' long side the
There lies your friend Tim Mc - Kin - ney. Can you take the news to his
Go fight the rest of the bat - tle for those who gave all they could
A G
grave. So,
wife?
give. I

you think the bat – tle is o – ver and you e – ven
No, son, the bat – tle's not o – ver. The bat – tle has
see, sir, the bat – tle's not o – ver. The bat – tle has

lay down your gun. You care – less – ly rise from your cov – er
on – ly be – gun. The rest of the bat – tle will cov – er
on – ly be – gun. The rest of the bat – tle will cov – er

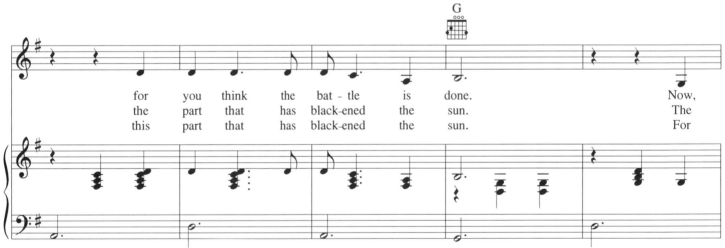

for you think the bat – tle is done. Now,
the part that has black-ened the sun. The
this part that has black-ened the sun. For

boy, hit the dirt, lis – ten to me, for I'm still the
fight yet to come's not the can-nons nor will the fight
though there's no sound of the can – non and though there's no

BIG RIVER

Words and Music by
JOHN R. CASH

With movement

Now, I taught the weep-ing wil-low how to cry,_____ And I showed the clouds how to cov-er up a clear blue sky. And the tears that I cried for that wom-an_____ are gon-na flood you Big Riv-er. Then I'm gon-na sit right here un-til I die. 2. I die._____

2. I met her accident'ly in St. Paul (Minnesota).
And it tore me up ev'ry time I heard her drawl, Southern drawl.
Then I heard my dream was back down stream cavortin' in Davenport,
And I followed you, Big River, when you called.

3. Then you took me to St. Louis later on (down the river).
A freighter said she's been here but she's gone, boy, she's gone.
I found her trail in Memphis, but she just walked up the block.
She raised a few eyebrows and then she went on down alone.

4. Now, won't you batter down by Baton Rouge, River Queen, roll it on.
Take that woman on down to New Orleans, New Orleans.
Go on, I've had enough; dump my blues down in the gulf.
She loves you, Big River, more than me.

Repeat 1st Verse

A BOY NAMED SUE

Words and Music by
SHEL SILVERSTEIN

Moderately bright

(Spoken)
1. Well, my "daddy" left home when I was three, and he didn't leave much to ma and me. Just this old guitar and an empty bottle of booze.

Now, I don't blame him because he run and hid, but the meanest thing that he ever did was be-

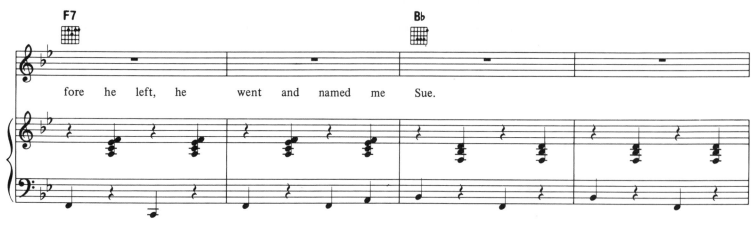

fore he left, he went and named me Sue.

Well, he must have thought it was quite a joke, And it got lots of laughs from a

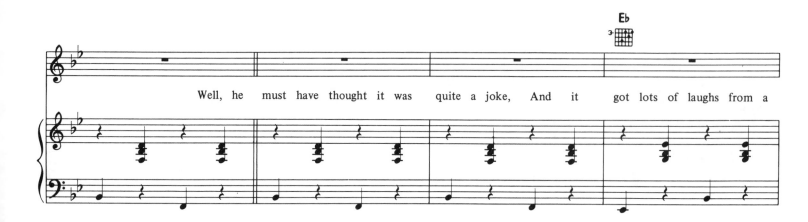

lot of folks. It seems I had to fight my whole life through.

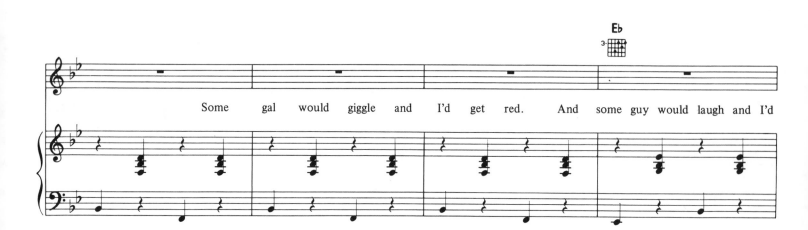

Some gal would giggle and I'd get red. And some guy would laugh and I'd

2. (Well,) I grew up quick and I grew up mean, My fist got hard and my wits got keen.
Roamed from town to town to hide my shame, but I made me a vow to the moon and stars,
I'd search the honky tonks and bars and kill that man that give me that awful name.

But it was Gatlinburg in mid July and I had just hit town and my throat was dry.
I'd thought I'd stop and have myself a brew. At an old saloon on a street of mud
And at a table dealing stud sat the dirty, mangy dog that named me Sue.

3. Well I knew that snake was my own sweet dad from a worn-out picture that my mother had.
And I know that scar on his cheek and his evil eye. He was big and bent and gray and old
And I looked at him and my blood ran cold, and I said "My name is Sue. How do you do.

Now you're gonna die. "Yeah, that's what I told him.

Well I hit him right between the eyes and he went down, but to my surprise he come up with a knife
And cut off a piece of my ear. But I busted a chair right across his teeth. And we crashed through
The wall and into the street kicking and a-gouging in the mud and the blood and the beer.

4. I tell you I've fought tougher men but I really can't remember when.
He kicked like a mule and he bit like a crocodile. I heard him laughin' and then I heard him cussin',
He went for his gun and I pulled mine first. He stood there looking at me and I saw him smile,

And he said, "Son, this world is rough and if a man's gonna make it, he's gotta be tough
And I know I wouldn't be there to help you along. So I give you that name and I said 'Goodbye,'
I knew you'd have to get tough or die. And it's that name that helped to make you strong.

5. Yeah, he said now you have just fought one helluva fight, and I know you hate me and you've
Got the right to kill me now and I wouldn't blame you if you do. But you ought to thank me
Before I die for the gravel in your guts and the spit in your eye because I'm the_ _ _ _
That named you Sue."

Yeah, what could I do? What could I do?

I got all choked up and I threw down my gun. Called him a pa and he called me a son,
And I come away with a different point of view. And I think about him now and then.
Every time I tried, every time I win and if I ever have a son I think I am gonna name him
Bill or George - - anything but Sue.

BUSTED

Words and Music by
HARLAN HOWARD

COME IN, STRANGER

Words and Music by
JOHN R. CASH

Moderately fast

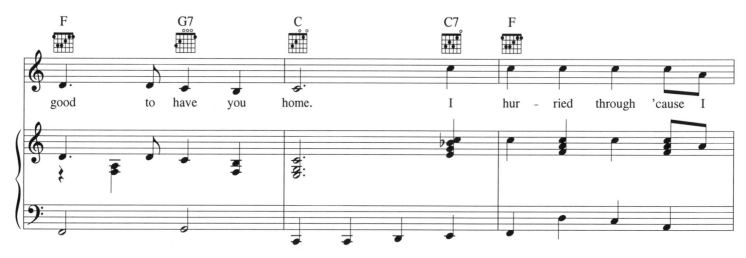

She said, "Come in, strang-er, it's good to have you home. I hur-ried through 'cause I

knew it was you, __ when I saw your dog wag-gin' his tail.

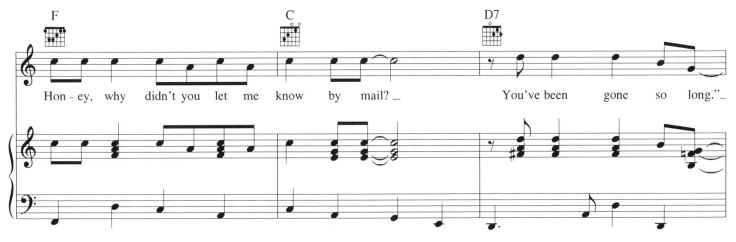

Hon - ey, why didn't you let me know by mail? _ You've been gone so long." _

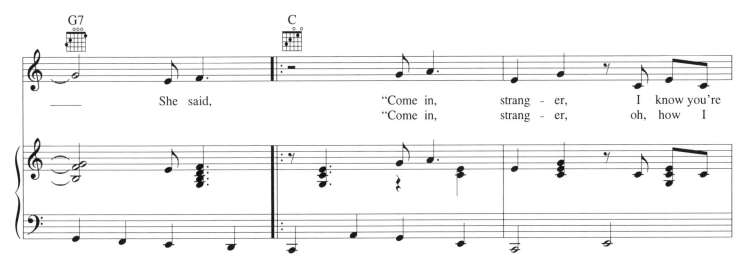

_____ She said, "Come in, strang - er, I know you're
"Come in, strang - er, oh, how I

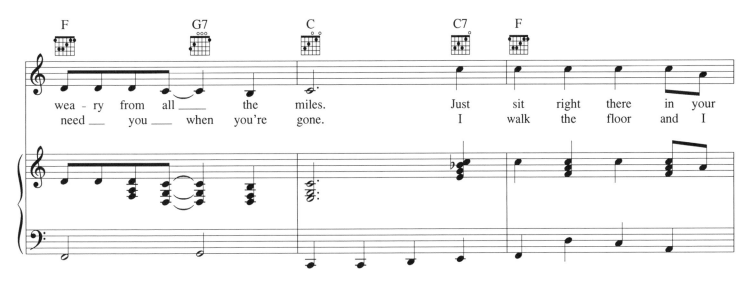

wea - ry from all _____ the miles. Just sit right there in your
need _ you _ when you're gone. I walk the there floor and I

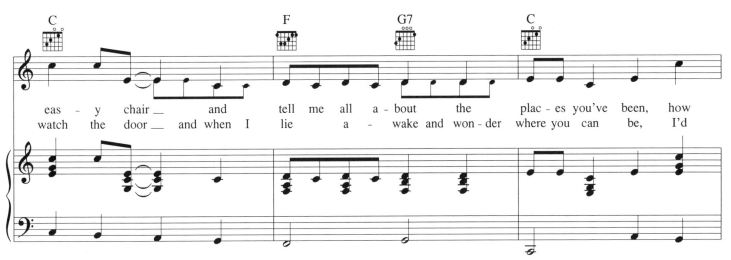

eas - y chair _ and tell me all a - bout the plac - es you've been, how
watch the door _ and when I lie a - wake and won - der where you can be, I'd

long it'll be ___ be - fore you leave a - gain. ___ I ___ hope it's a long, long while." ___
give an - y - thing to have you here with me. I get so lone - some ___ all a - lone." ___

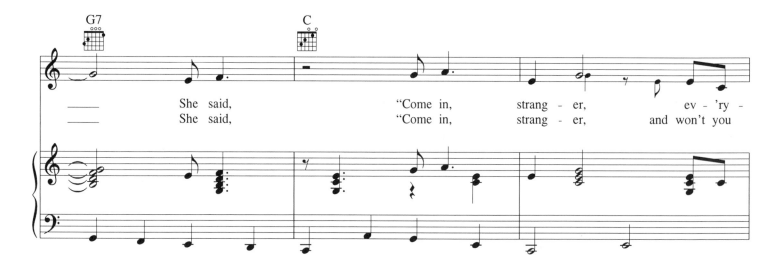

___ She said, "Come in, strang - er, ev - 'ry -
___ She said, "Come in, strang - er, and won't you

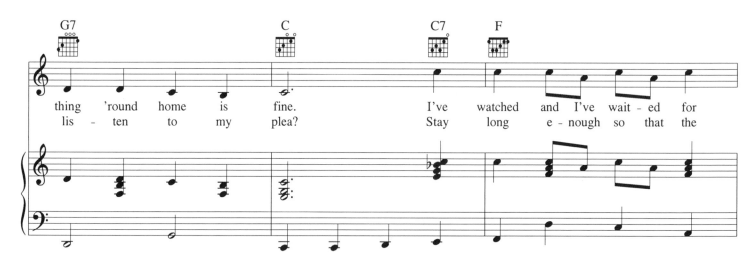

thing 'round home is fine. I've watched and I've wait - ed for
lis - ten to my plea? Stay long e - nough so that the

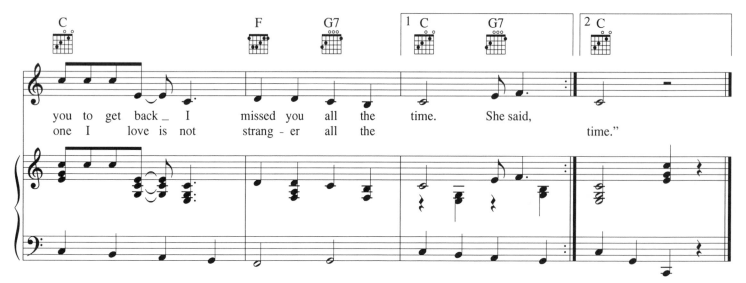

you to get back ___ I missed you all the time. She said,
one I love is not strang - er all the time."

DARK AS A DUNGEON

Words and Music by
MERLE TRAVIS

44

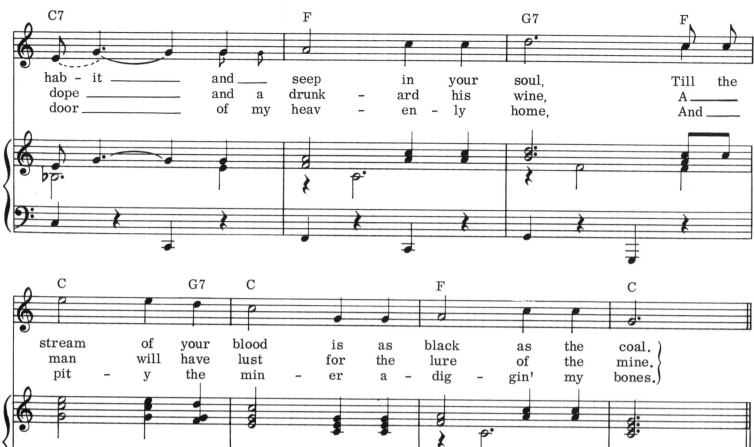

hab - it _____ and _____ seep in your soul, Till the
dope _____ and a drunk - ard his wine, A _____
door _____ of my heav - en - ly home, And _____

stream of your blood is as black as the coal.
man will have lust for the lure of the mine.
pit - y the min - er a - dig - gin' my bones.

Refrain

It's dark as a dun - geon and damp as the

dew, Where dan - ger is dou - ble _____ and pleas - ures are

few, Where the rain nev-er falls and the sun nev-er

shines, It's dark as a dun-geon 'way down in the

1.

mine. 2. It's
3. I

2.

mine.

CRY, CRY, CRY

Words and Music by
JOHN R. CASH

F7/A

time when I would try, try, try, 'Cause

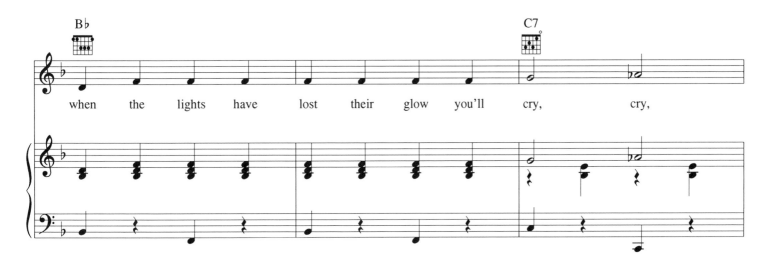

B♭   C7

when the lights have lost their glow you'll cry, cry,

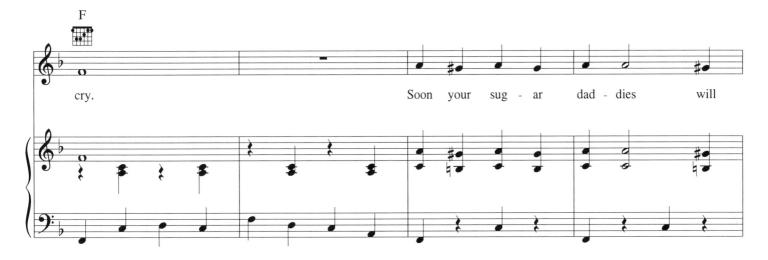

F

cry.   Soon your sug-ar dad-dies will

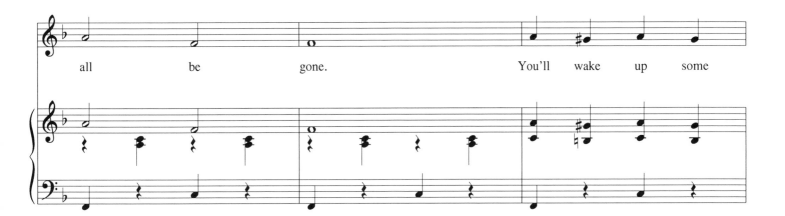

all be gone. You'll wake up some

cold day and find you're a - lone. You'll

call for me, but I'm gon - na tell you bye, bye,

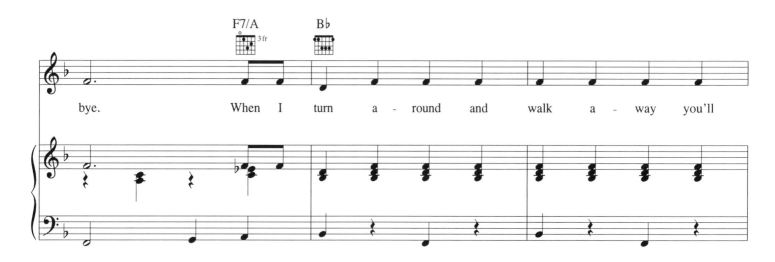

bye. When I turn a - round and walk a - way you'll

cry, cry, cry. _____ You're gon - na cry, cry,

cry, and you cry a - lone. When ev - 'ry - one's for -

got - ten and you're left on your own, you're gon - na

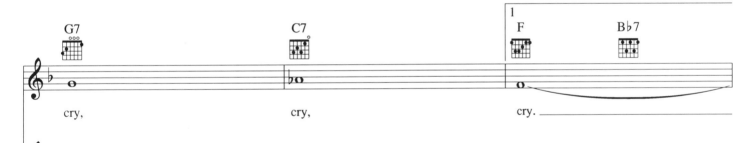

cry, cry, cry.

___ Ev - 'ry - bod - y cry. ___

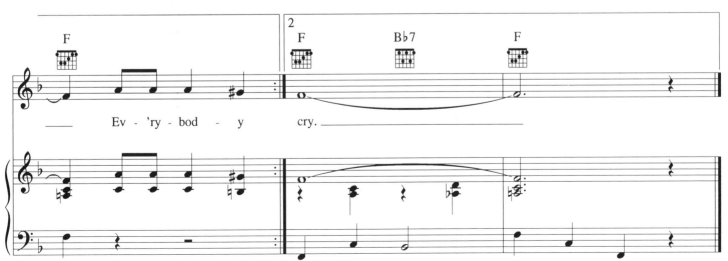

DADDY SANG BASS

Words and Music by
CARL PERKINS

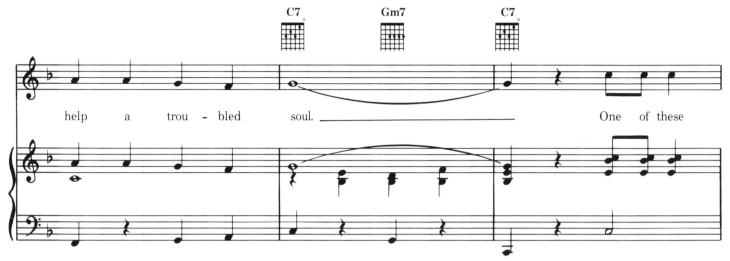

help a trou - bled soul. _____ One of these

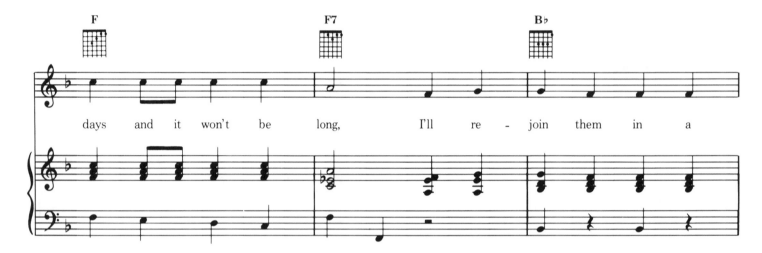

days and it won't be long, I'll re - join them in a

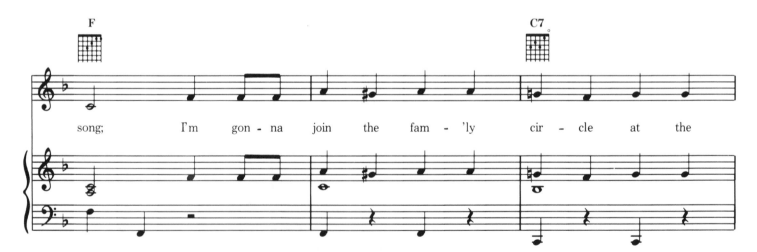

song; I'm gon - na join the fam - 'ly cir - cle at the

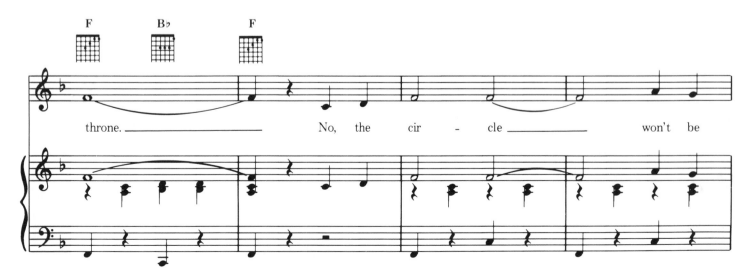

throne. _____ No, the cir - cle _____ won't be

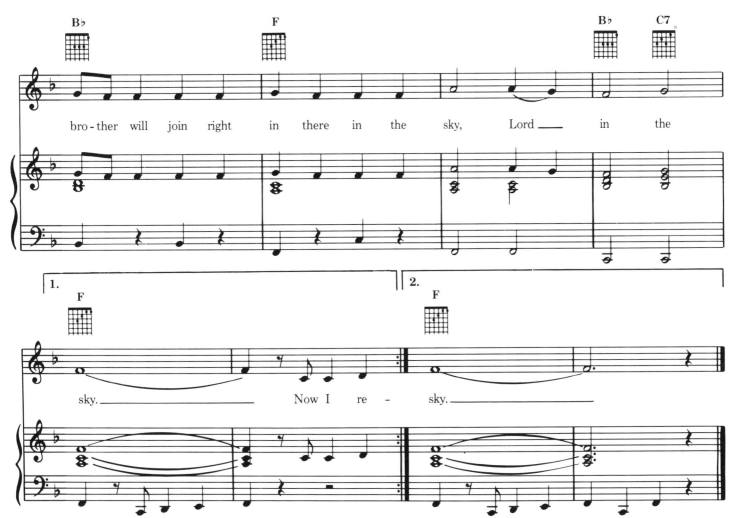

DON'T TAKE YOUR GUNS TO TOWN

Words and Music by
JOHNNY R. CASH

Moderately

1. A

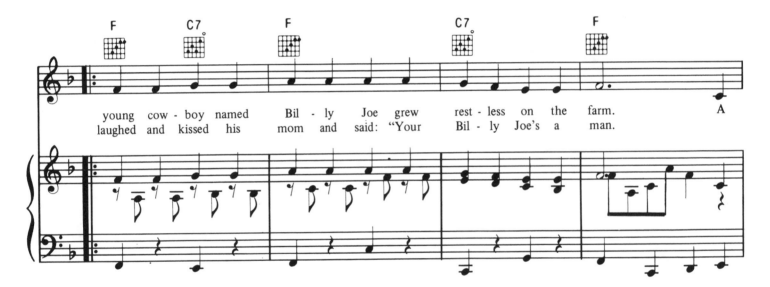

young cow-boy named Bil-ly Joe grew rest-less on the farm.
laughed and kissed his mom and said: "Your Bil-ly Joe's a man.

A

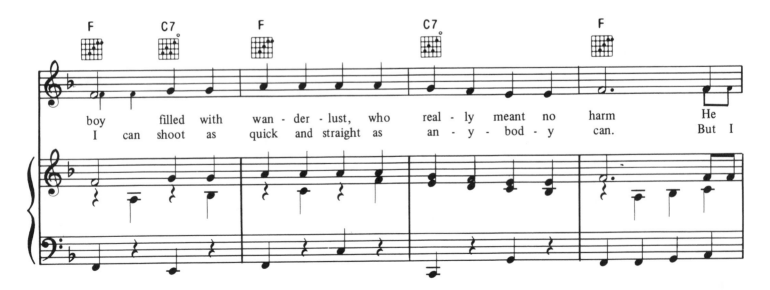

boy filled with wan-der-lust, who real-ly meant no harm He
I can shoot as quick and straight as an-y-bod-y can. But I

3. He sang a song as on he rode, his guns hung at his hips.
   He rode into a cattle town, a smile upon his lips.
   He stopped and walked into a bar and laid his money down,
   But his mother's words echoed again:"Don't Take Your Guns To Town, son;
   Leave your guns at home, Bill; Don't Take Your Guns To Town."

4. He drank his first strong liquor then to calm his shaking hand,
   And tried to tell himself at last he had become a man.
   A dusty cowpoke at his side began to laugh him down.
   And he heard again his mother's words: "Don't Take Your Guns To Town, son;
   Leave your guns at home, Bill; Don't Take Your Guns To Town."

5. Bill was raged and Billy Joe reached for his gun to draw.
   But the stranger drew his gun and fired before he even saw.
   As Billy Joe fell to the floor the crowd all gathered 'round
   And wondered at his final words: "Don't Take Your Guns To Town, son;
   Leave your guns at home, Bill; Don't Take Your Guns To Town."

FIVE FEET HIGH AND RISING

Words and Music by
JOHNNY CASH

Moderately

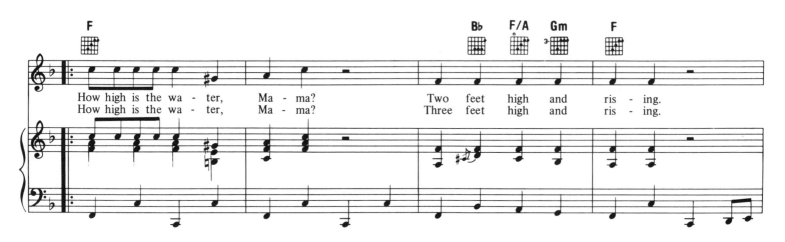

How high is the wa-ter, Ma-ma? Two feet high and ris - ing.
How high is the wa-ter, Ma-ma? Three feet high and ris - ing.

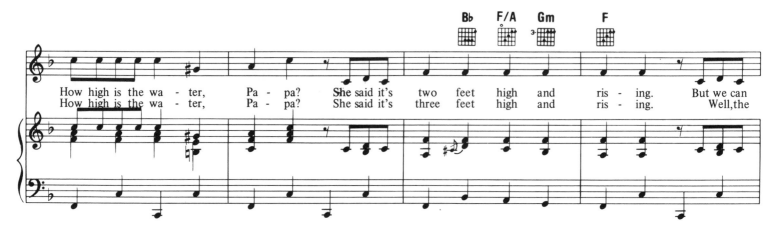

How high is the wa-ter, Pa-pa? She said it's two feet high and ris - ing. But we can
How high is the wa-ter, Pa-pa? She said it's three feet high and ris - ing. Well, the

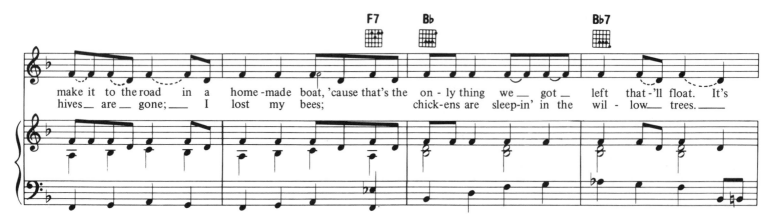

make it to the road in a home-made boat, 'cause that's the on - ly thing we got left that-'ll float. It's
hives are gone; I lost my bees; chick-ens are sleep-in' in the wil - low trees.

al - read -y o -ver all the wheat and oats.   Two feet high and ris - ing.
cows in __ wa -ter up __ past their knees.   Three feet high and ris - ing.

ris - ing,   well it's Five Feet High And Ris - ing.

3. How high is the water, Mama? Four feet high and rising.
    How high is the water, Papa? She said it's four feet high and rising.
    Hey, come look through the window pane; the bus is comin' gonna take us to the train.
    Looks like we'll be blessed with a little more rain. Four feet high and rising.

4. How high is the water, Mama? Five Feet High And Rising.
    How high is the water, Papa? She said it's Five Feet High And Rising.
    Well, the rails are washed out north of town; we gotta head for higher ground.
    We can't come back till the water goes down. Five Feet High And Rising;
    Well, it's Five Feet High And Rising.

FLESH AND BLOOD

Words and Music by
JOHN R. CASH

Be- side a singin' moun- tain stream where the pus- sy wil- low grew
leaned a- gainst the bark of a birch and I breathed the hon- ey dew. Where

sil- ver leaf of ma- ple spar- kled in the morn- ing dew I
Saw a north- bound flock of geese a- gainst the sky of ba- by blue. A-

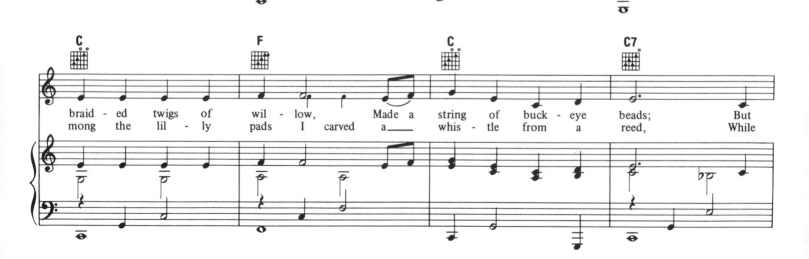

braid- ed twigs of wil- low, Made a string of buck- eye beads; But
mong the lil- ly pads I carved a___ whis- tle from a reed, While

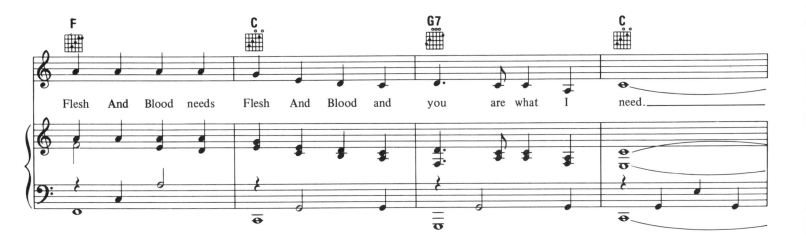

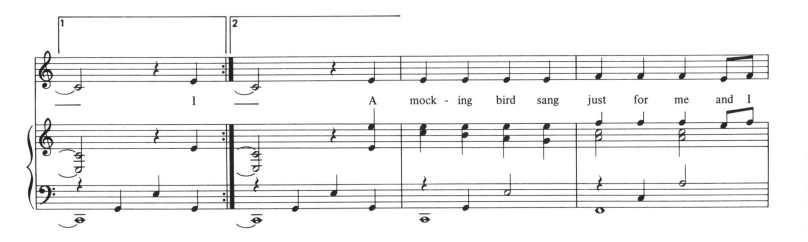

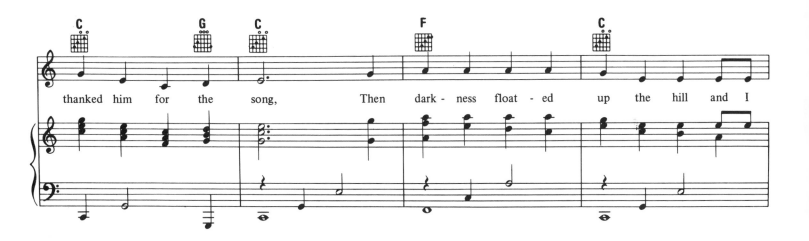

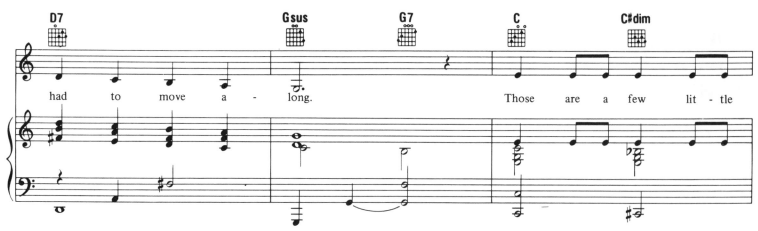

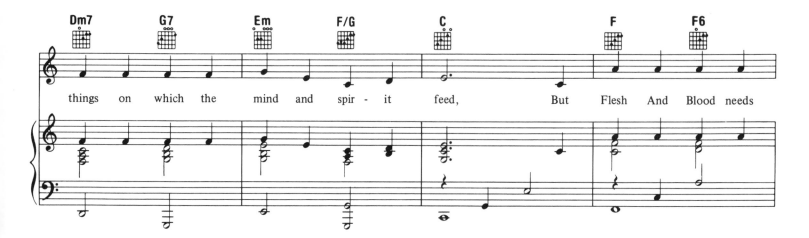

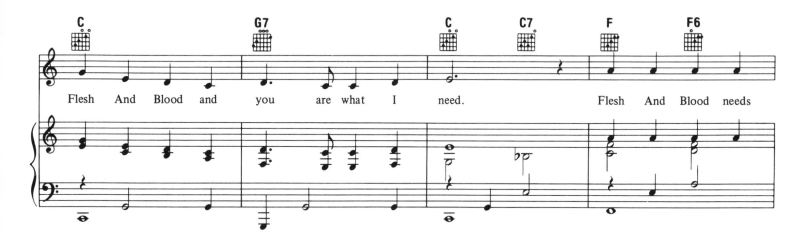

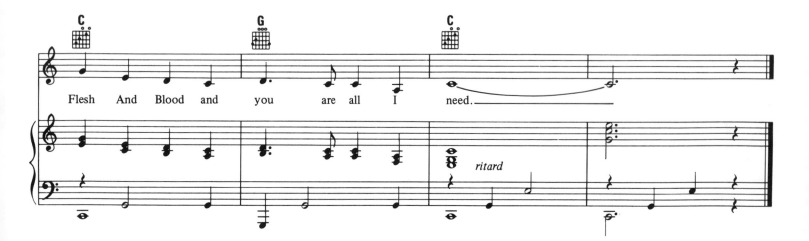

GIVE MY LOVE TO ROSE

Words and Music by
JOHN R. CASH

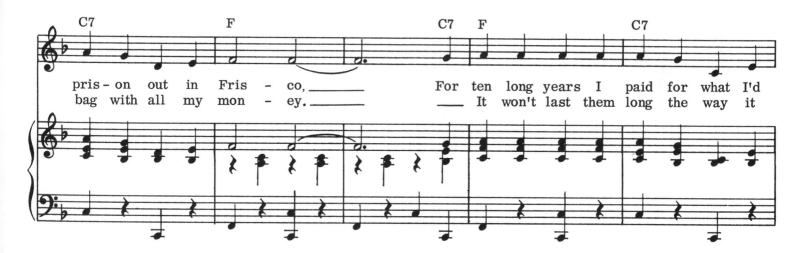

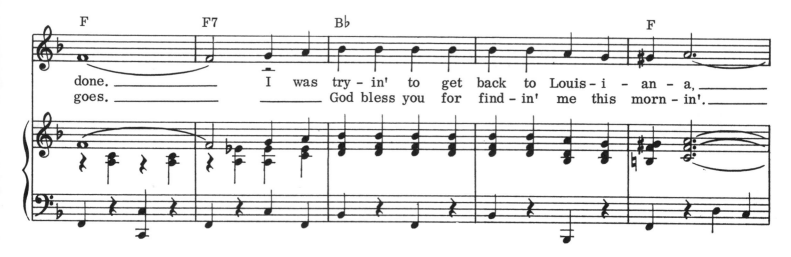

Chorus

Give my love to Rose, please, won't you, mis - ter? _____

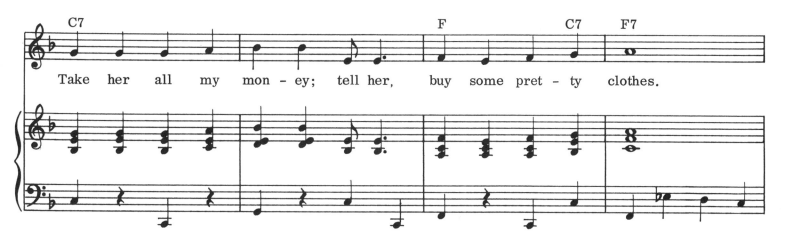

Take her all my mon - ey; tell her, buy some pret - ty clothes.

Tell my boy that Dad-dy's so proud of him _____ And don't for-get to

give my love to Rose. _____ 2. Won't-cha Rose. _____

FOLSOM PRISON BLUES

Words and Music by
JOHN R. CASH

Moderately (not too slow)

Chorus

1. I

hear the train a - com - in'; it's roll - in' 'round the bend, And

I was just a ba - by my ma - ma told me son, _____

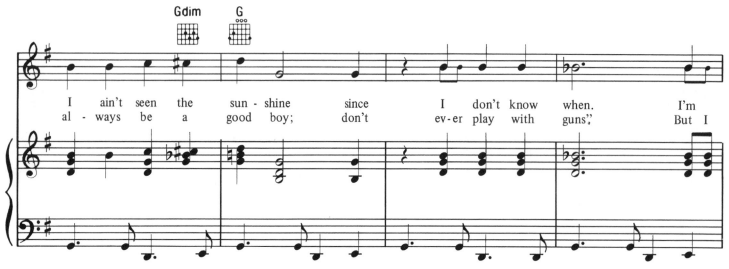

I ain't seen the sun - shine since I don't know when. I'm

al - ways be a good boy; don't ev - er play with guns,' But I

stuck at Fol - som Pris - on and time keeps drag - gin' on.
shot a man in Re - no just ___ to watch him die.

But that train keeps roll - in'
When I hear that whis - tle blow - in'

on down to San ___ An - tone. ___ When ___
I hang my head ___ and ___ cry. ___

3. I bet there's rich folks eatin' in a fancy dining car.
   They're prob'ly drinkin' coffee and smokin' big cigars,
   But I know I had it comin', I know I can't be free,
   But those people keep a-movin', and that's what tortures me.

4. Well, if they freed me from this prison, if that railroad train was mine,
   I bet I'd move on over a little farther down the line,
   Far from Folsom Prison, that's where I want to stay,
   And I'd let that lonesome whistle blow my blues away.

FRANKIE'S MAN, JOHNNY

Words and Music by
JOHNNY R. CASH

1. Now, Frank-ie and John-ny were sweet-hearts. They were true as a blue blue sky. He was a long-leg-ged gui-tar pick-er with a wick-ed wan-der-in' eye. But he was her man

2. Well, John-ny he packed up to leave her, But he prom-ised he'd be back. He said he had a lit-tle pick-in' to do a lit-tle far-ther down the track. He said: "I am your man;

3. Well, Frankie curled up on the sofa, thinkin' about her man.

   Far away the couples were dancin' to the music of his band.

   He was Frankie's man; he wasn't doin' her wrong.

4. Then in the front door walked a redhead; Johnny saw her right away.

   She came down by the bandstand to watch him while he played.

   He was Frankie's man, but she was far away.

5. He sang every song to the redhead; she smiled back at him.

   Then he came and sat at her table, where the lights were low and dim.

   What Frankie didn't know wouldn't hurt her none.

6. Then the redhead jumped up and slapped him; she slapped him a time or two.

   She said, "I'm Frankie's sister, and I was checkin' up on you.

   If you're her man, you better treat her right."

7. Well, the moral of this story is: be good but carry a stick.

   Sometimes it looks like a guitar picker just can't tell what to pick.

   He was Frankie's man, and he still ain't done her wrong.

GUESS THINGS HAPPEN THAT WAY

Words and Music by
JACK CLEMENT

Moderately

mp

CHORUS

1. You ask me if I'll for-get my ba-by. I guess I will some day.
2. You ask me if I'll miss her kiss-es. I guess I will ev-'ry day.

I don't like it but I guess things hap-pen that way. You / You

ask me if I'll get a-long. I guess I will some way.
ask me if I'll find an-oth-er. I don't know; I can't say.

I don't like it but I guess things hap-pen that way. _____

God gave me that girl to lean on; Then He put me on my own. _____

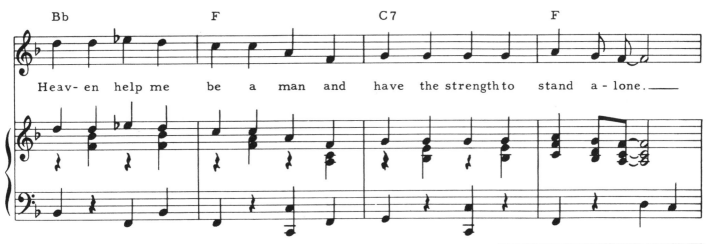

Heav-en help me be a man and have the strength to stand a-lone. _____

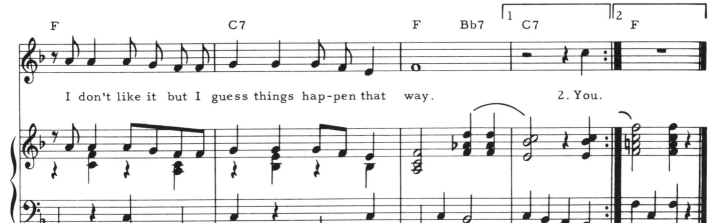

I don't like it but I guess things hap-pen that way.   2. You.

HEY, PORTER

Words and Music by
JOHN R. CASH

Fast country train beat

Hey,

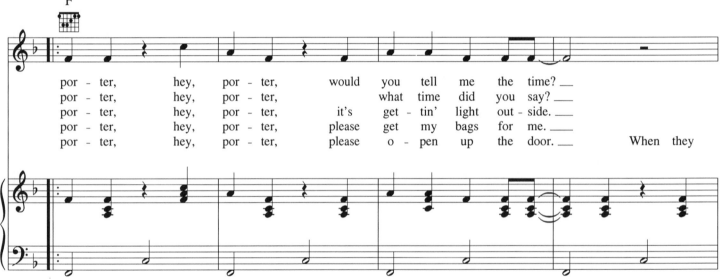

por - ter,	hey,	por - ter,	would	you	tell	me	the	time?
por - ter,	hey,	por - ter,	what	time	did	you	say?
por - ter,	hey,	por - ter,	it's	get - tin'	light	out - side.
por - ter,	hey,	por - ter,	please	get	my	bags	for	me.
por - ter,	hey,	por - ter,	please	o - pen	up	the	door.	When they

How much	long - er	will it	be	'til we	cross	that	Ma - son	Dix - on
How much	long - er	will it	be	'til I	can	see	the	light of
This ol'	train	is	puff - in'	smoke	and I	have	to	strain my
I need	no - bod - y	to	tell me	now	that	we're	in	Ten - nes -
stop this	train	I'm gon - na	get off	first	'cause	I	can't	wait no

line? At day - light would you tell that en - gi - neer to slow it
day? When we hit Dix - ie would you tell that en - gi - neer to ring his
eyes. But ask that en - gi - neer if he __ will blow his whis - tle,
see. Go tell that en - gi - neer to make __ that lone - some whis - tle
more. Tell that en - gi - neer I said thanks a lot ___ and I did - n't mind the

down, or bet - ter still, __ just stop the train __ 'cause I wan - na look a -
bell and ask ev - 'ry - bod - y that ain't a - sleep __ to stand right __ up and
please, 'cause I smell frost __ on cot - ton leaves __ and I feel that __ south - ern
scream. We're not so far __ from home, so take __ it eas - y ___ on the
fare. I'm gon - na set my feet __ on south - ern soil ___ and breathe that __ south - ern

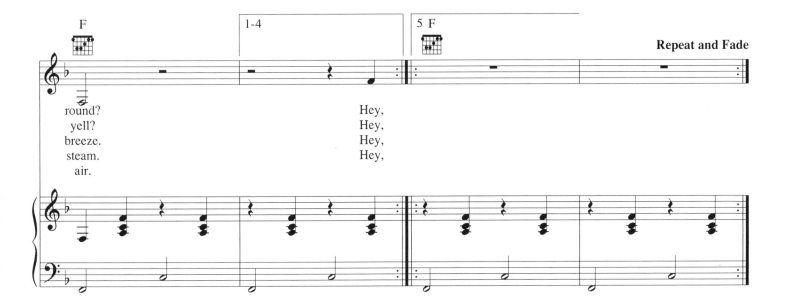

round? Hey,
yell? Hey,
breeze. Hey,
steam. Hey,
air.

I GOT STRIPES

New Words and New Music Arrangement by JOHNNY R. CASH
and CHARLIE WILLIAMS
Based on a song Collected, Adapted and Arranged by JOHN A. LOMAX
and ALAN LOMAX

Moderately

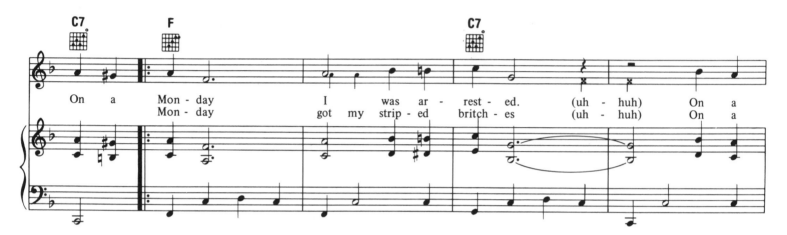

On a Mon-day I was ar-rest-ed. (uh-huh) On a
Mon-day got my strip-ed britch-es (uh-huh) On a

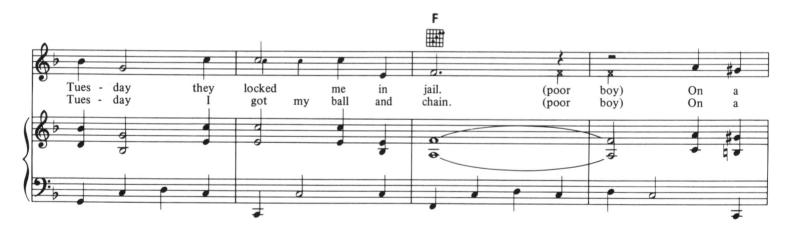

Tues-day they locked me in jail. (poor boy) On a
Tues-day I got my ball and chain. (poor boy) On a

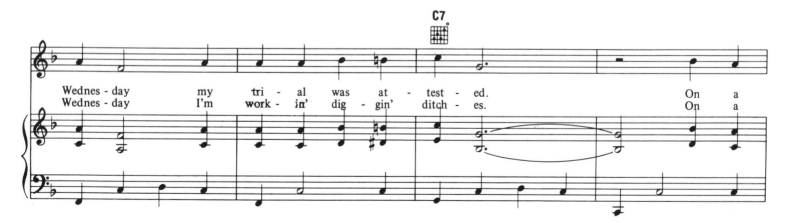

Wednes-day my tri-al was at-test-ed. On a
Wednes-day I'm work-in' dig-gin' ditch-es. On

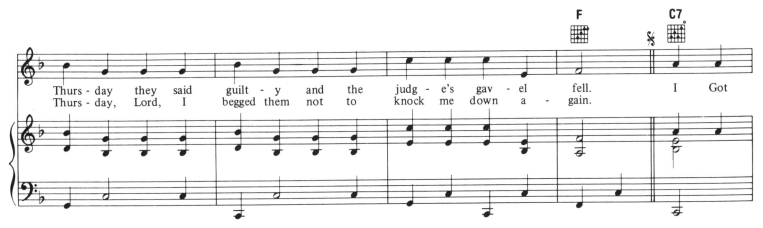

Thurs - day they said guilt - y and the judg - e's gav - el fell. I Got
Thurs - day, Lord, I begged them not to knock me down a - gain.

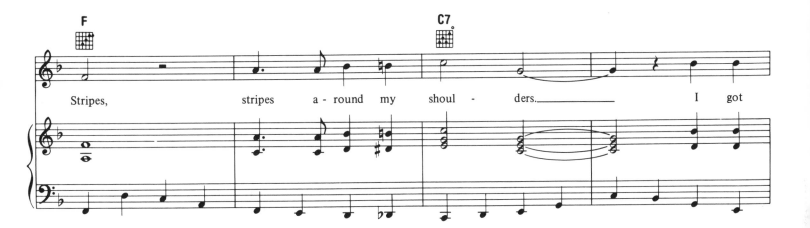

Stripes, stripes a - round my shoul - ders._____ I got

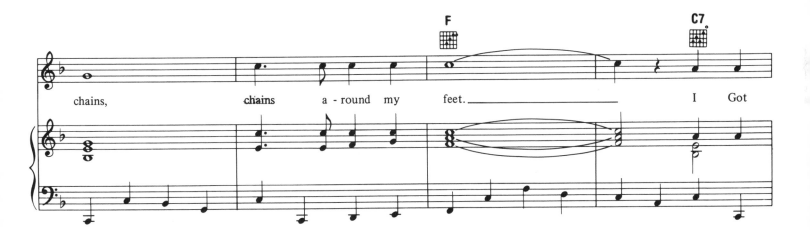

chains, chains a - round my feet._____ I Got

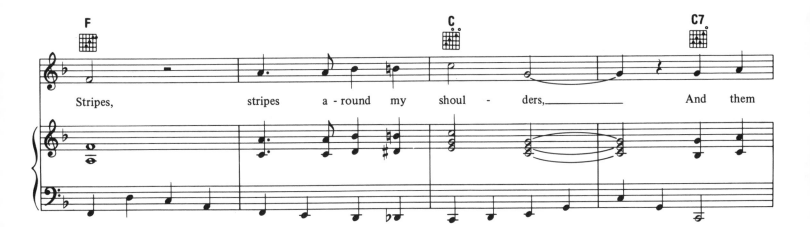

Stripes, stripes a - round my shoul - ders,_____ And them

JACKSON

Words and Music by BILLY EDD WHEELER
and JERRY LEIBER

I WALK THE LINE

Words and Music by
JOHN R. CASH

Moderate

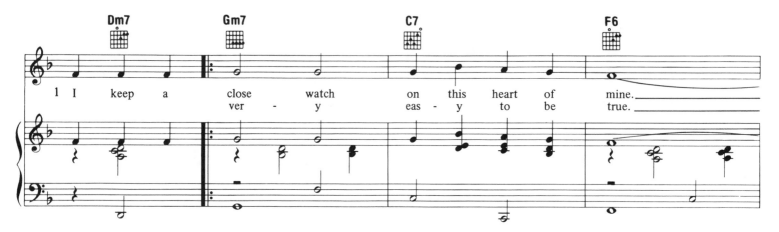

1. I keep a close watch on this heart of mine. _____
   ver - y eas - y to be true. _____

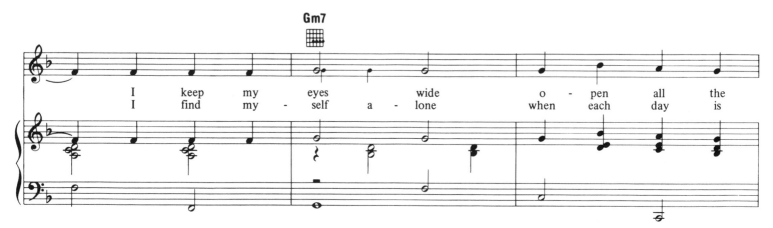

I keep my eyes wide o - pen all the
I find my - self a - lone when each day is

time. _____ I keep the' ends out for the tie that
through. _____ Yes, I'll ad - mit out that I'm a fool for

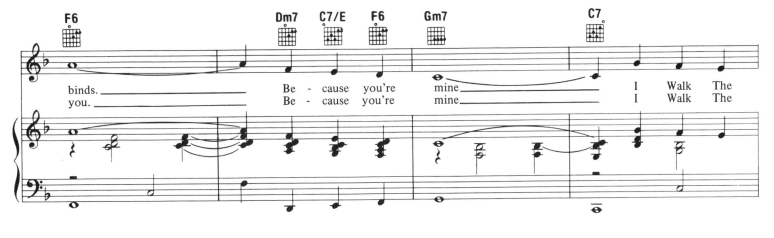

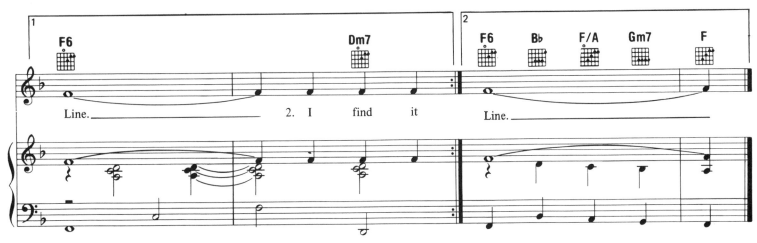

3. As sure as night is dark and day is light,
   I keep you on my mind both day and night.
   And happiness I've known proves that it's right.
   Because you're mine I Walk The Line.

4. You've got a way to keep me on your side.
   You give me cause for love that I can't hide.
   For you I know I'd even try to turn the tide.
   Because you're mine I Walk The Line.

5. I keep a close watch on this heart of mine.
   I keep my eyes wide open all the time.
   I keep the ends out for the tie that binds.
   Because you're mine I Walk The Line.

I WILL ROCK AND ROLL WITH YOU

Words and Music by
JOHN R. CASH

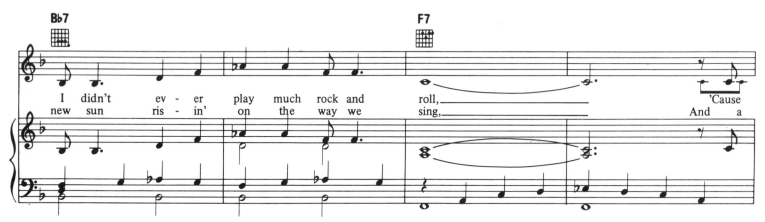

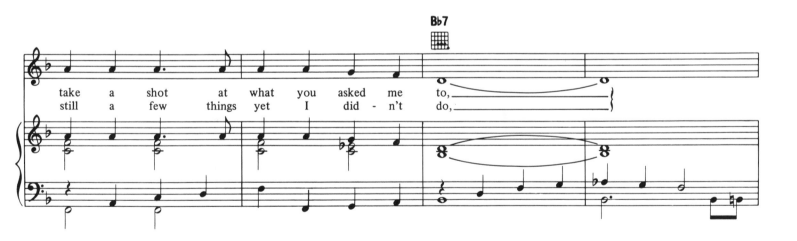

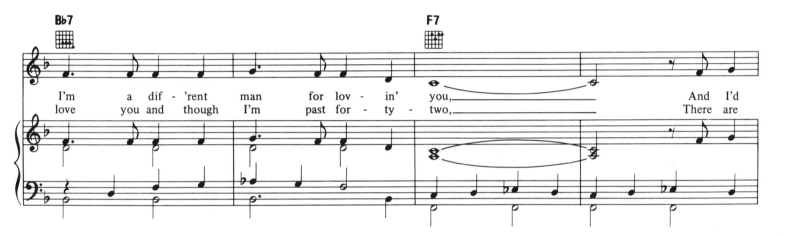

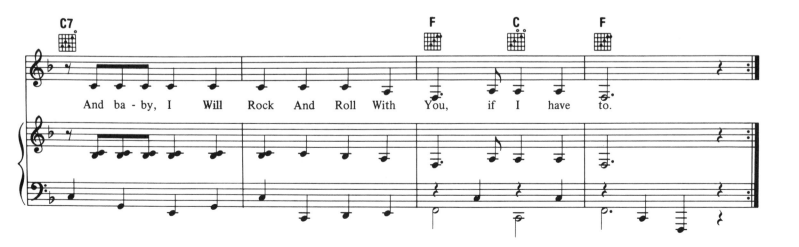

THE LAST TIME

Words and Music by
KRIS KRISTOFFERSON

Moderately

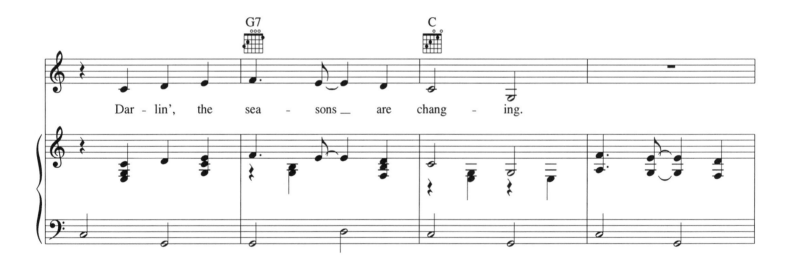

Dar - lin', the sea - sons __ are chang - ing.

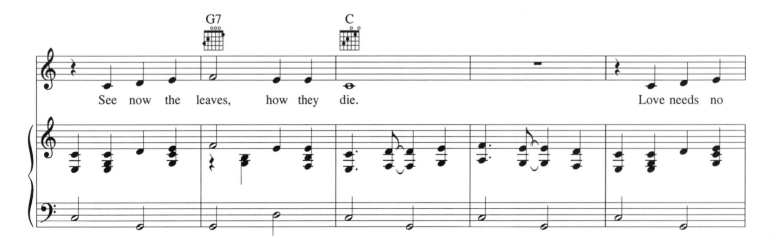

See now the leaves, how they die.

Love needs no

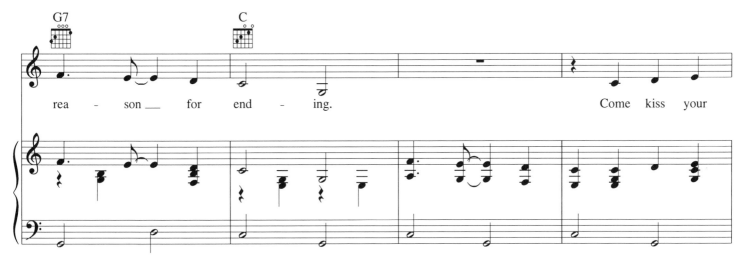

rea - son __ for end - ing.   Come kiss your

ba - by __ good - bye.   Dar - lin', the
                                       Now and a -

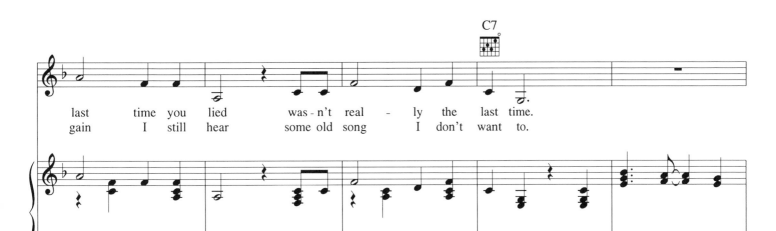

last   time you   lied   was-n't real - ly the last time.
gain   I   still hear   some old song   I don't want to.

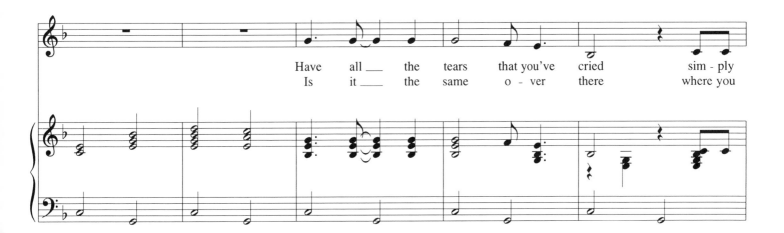

Have   all __ the tears   that you've   cried   sim - ply
Is   it __ the same   o - ver   there   where you

dried up and gone?
found your new friend?

All in the world you can hurt an - y -
Some - times at night I still wake up and ___

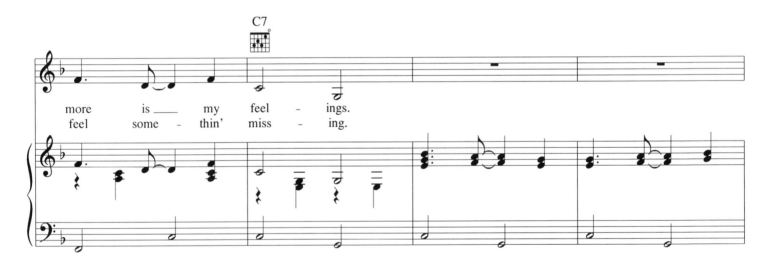

more is ___ my feel - ings.
feel some - thin' miss - ing.

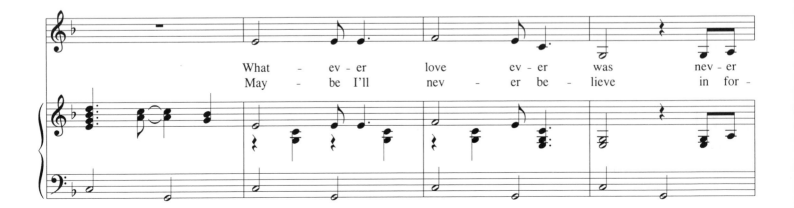

What - ev - er love ev - er was nev - er
May - be I'll nev - er be - lieve in for -

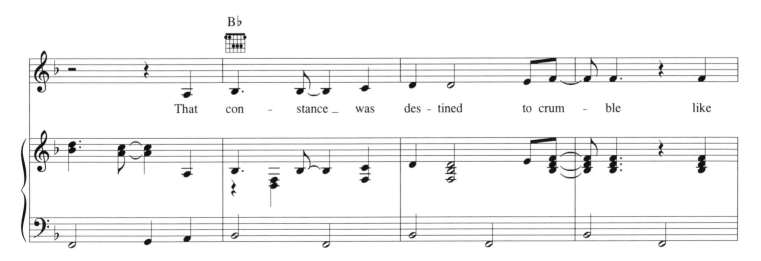

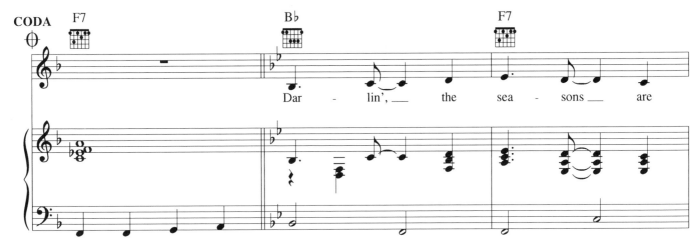

LUTHER'S BOOGIE
(Luther Played the Boogie)

Words and Music by
JOHN R. CASH

Moderately fast

We were just a plain ol' hill-bill-y band
did our best to en-ter-tain ev'ry-

_____ with a plain ol' coun-try style. We nev-er played the kind of
where plain we'd go. We'd near-ly wear our

songs that would drive an-y-bod-y wild. Played a
fin-gers off to give the folks a show. Played

rail - road song ___ with a stomp - in' beat, ___ we played a blues song, kind - a
jump - in' jack ___ to make 'em get in a groove, _ we played sad songs kind - a real ___

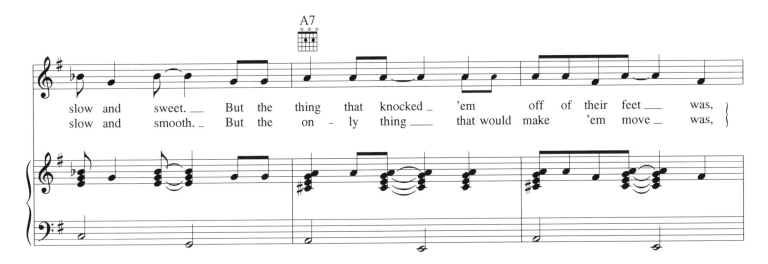

slow and sweet. ___ But the thing that knocked ___ 'em off of their feet ___ was,
slow and smooth. _ But the on - ly thing ___ that would make 'em move ___ was,

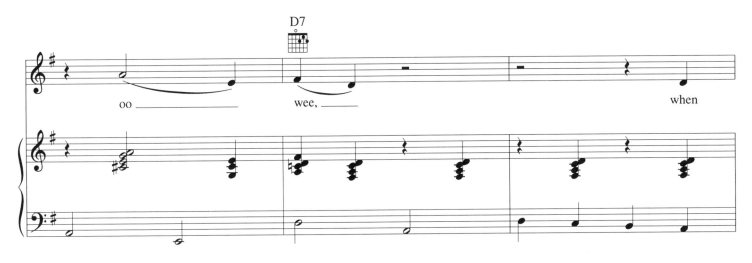

oo _____ wee, _____ when

Lu - ther played the boo - gie woo - gie, Lu - ther played the boo - gie woo - gie, Lu - ther played the boo - gie woo - gie,

Lu - ther played the boo - gie woo - gie, Lu - ther played the boo - gie woo - gie, Lu - ther played the boo - gie woo - gie,

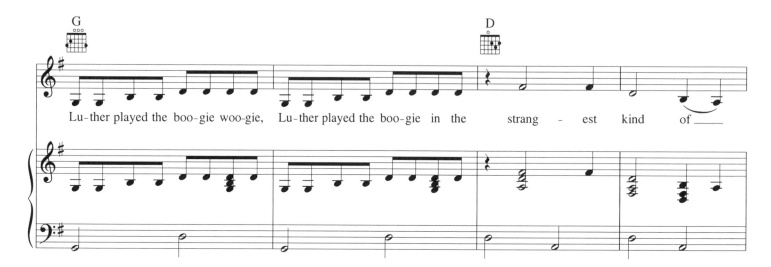

Lu - ther played the boo - gie woo - gie, Lu - ther played the boo - gie in the strang - est kind of ____

way.

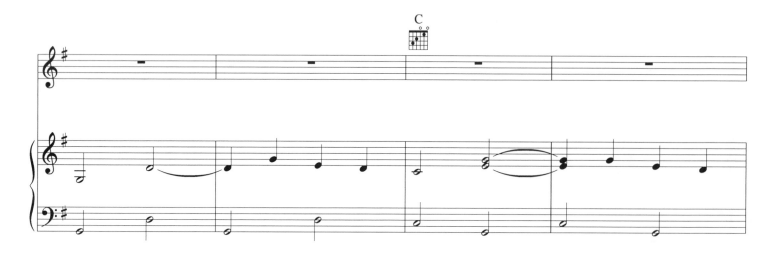

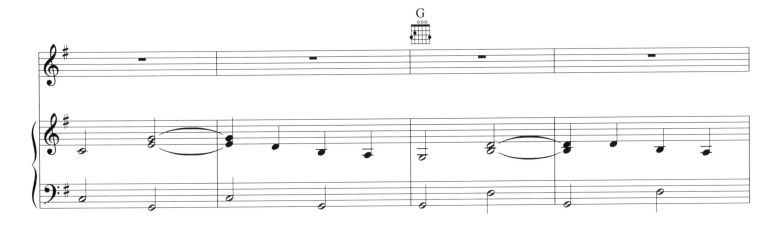

Well, we   (Spoken:) Now, didn't Luther play the boogie strange?

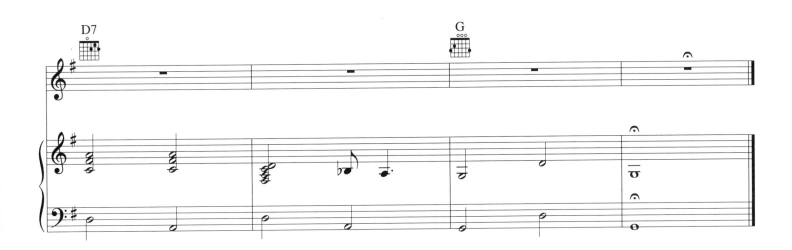

THE MAN IN BLACK

Words and Music by
JOHN R. CASH

Moderately

Well, you won-der why I al-ways dress in black, _____ Why you
wear the black for ___ those who nev-er read ___ Or

nev-er see bright col-ors on my back, _____ And
lis-tened to the words that Je-sus said _____ A-

why does my ap-pear-ance seem to have a som-ber tone. Well there's a
bout the road to hap-pi-ness thru have love and char-i-ty. Why you'd

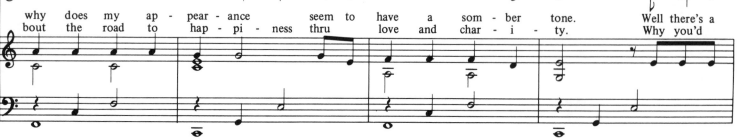

93

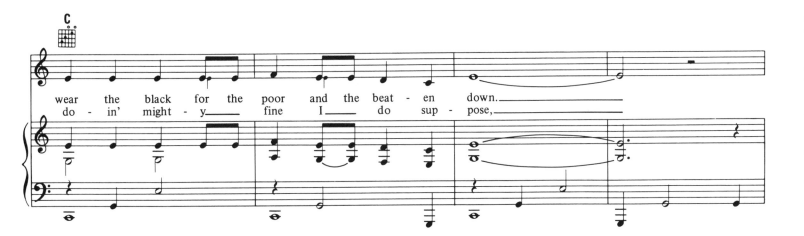

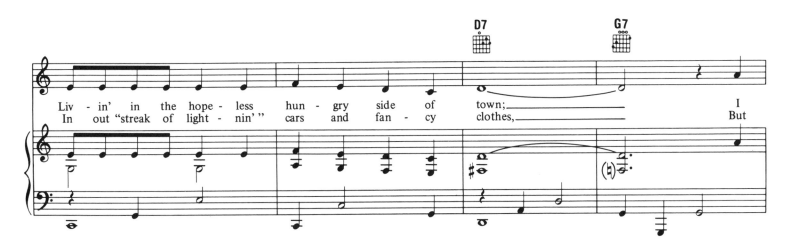

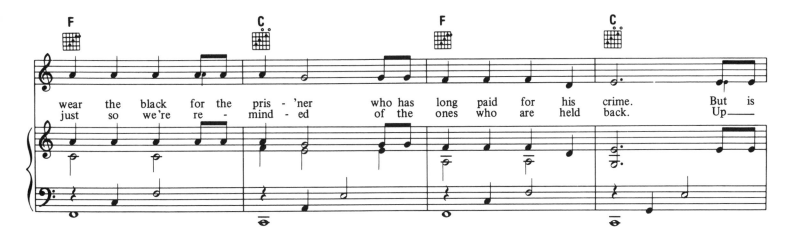

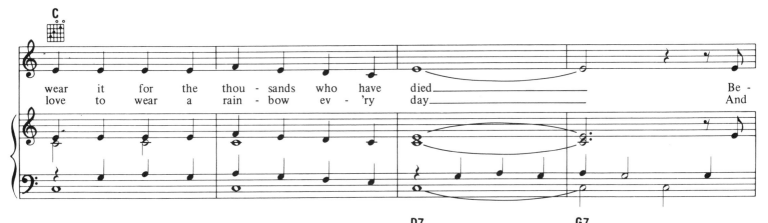

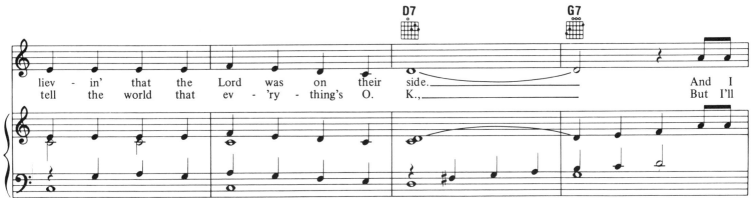

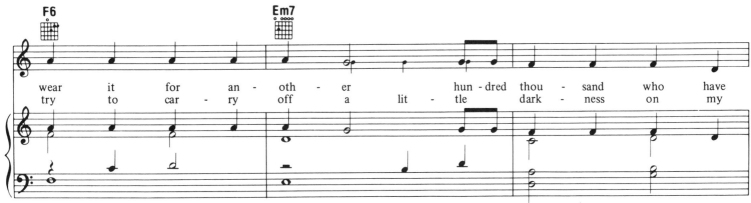

ONE PIECE AT A TIME

Words and Music by
WAYNE KEMP

Talking blues tempo

1. Well I

left Ken-tuck-y back in for-ty nine and went to De-troit work-in' on as-sem-bly lines. The

first year, they had me put-tin' wheels on Cad-il - lacs. Ev-'ry

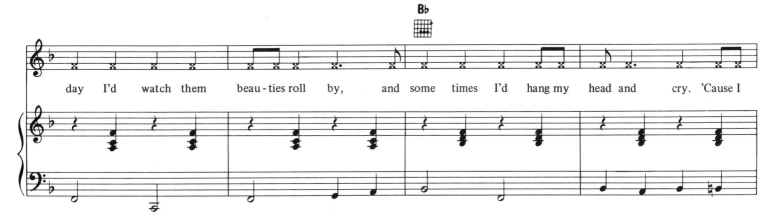

day I'd watch them beau-ties roll by, and some times I'd hang my head and cry. 'Cause I

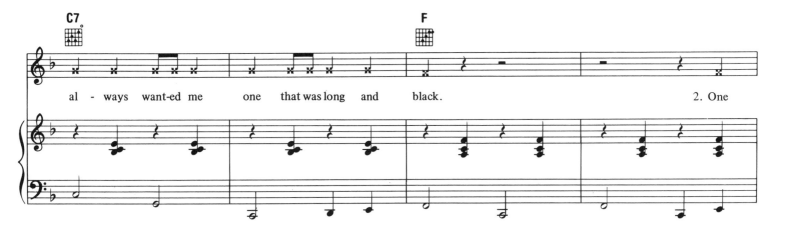

al - ways want-ed me one that was long and black. 2. One

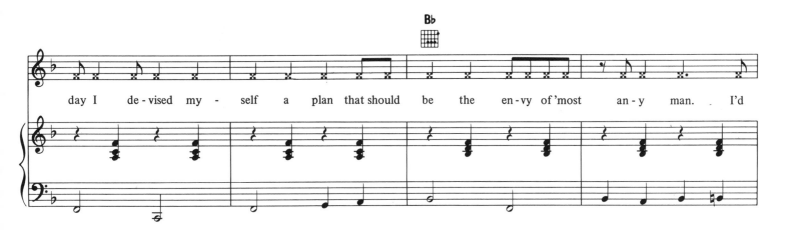

day I de-vised my - self a plan that should be the en-vy of 'most an-y man. I'd

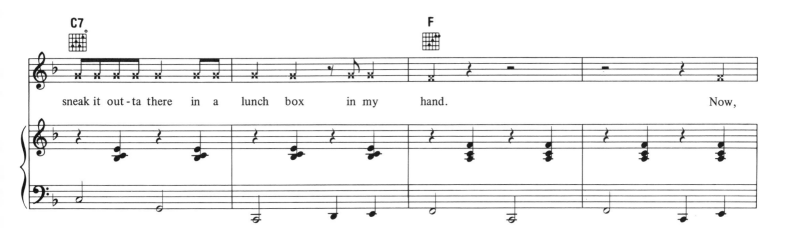

sneak it out-ta there in a lunch box in my hand. Now,

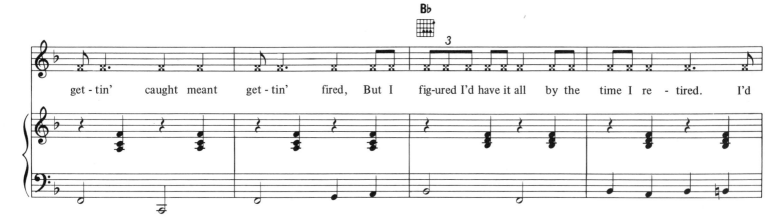

get-tin' caught meant get-tin' fired, But I fig-ured I'd have it all by the time I re-tired. I'd

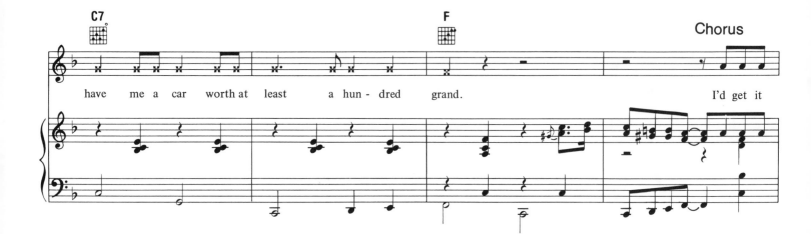

have me a car worth at least a hun-dred grand. I'd get it

One Piece At A Time and it would-n't cost me a dime, you'd

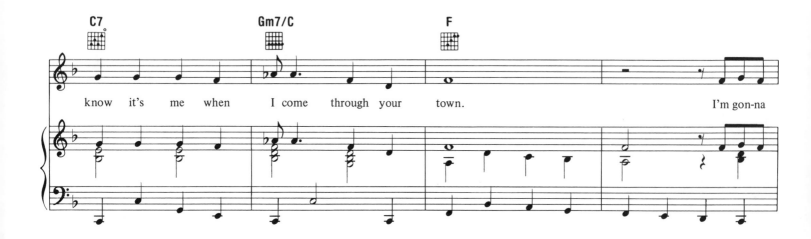

know it's me when I come through your town. I'm gon-na

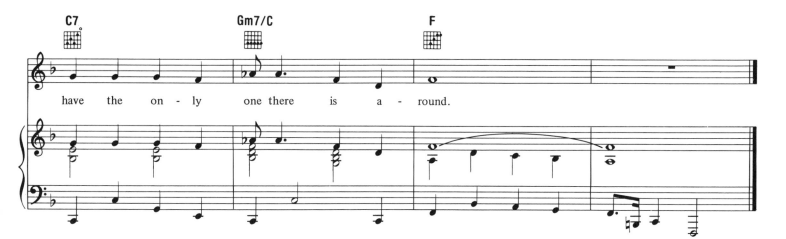

RECITATION

3. So, the very next day when I punched in with my big lunch box
And with help from my friends, I left that day with a lunch box full of gears.
I've never considered myself a thief, but GM wouldn't miss just one little piece
Especially if I strung it out over several years.

4. The first day, I got me a fuel pump, and the next day I got me an engine and a trunk.
Then, I got me a transmission and all the chrome.
The little things I could get in the big lunch box
Like nuts and bolts and all four shocks.
But the big stuff we snuck out in my buddy's mobile home.

5. Now, up to now, my plan went all right, 'til we tried to put it all together one night.
And that's when we noticed that something was definitely wrong.
The transmission was a '53, and the motor turned out to be a '73,
And when we tried to put in the bolts, all the holes were gone.
So, we drilled it out so that it would fit, and with a little bit of help from an adapter kit,
We had the engine running just like a song.

6. Now the headlights, they was another sight,
We had two on the left, and one on the right.
But when we pulled out the switch, all three of 'em come on.
The back end looked kinda funny, too.
But we put it together, and when we got through, well, that's when we noticed that we only had one tail fin.
About that time, my wife walked out, and I could see in her eyes that she had her doubts.
But she opened the door and said, "Honey, take me for a spin."

7. So, we drove uptown just to get the tags, and I headed her right on down the main drag.
I could hear everybody laughin' for blocks around.
But, up there at the court house, they didn't laugh,
'Cause to type it up, it took the whole staff.
And when they got through, the title weighed sixty pounds.

2nd CHORUS: I got it One Piece At A Time, and it didn't cost me a dime.
You'll know it's me when I come through your town.
I'm gonna ride around in style; I'm gonna drive everybody wild,
'Cause I'll have the only one there is around.

(Ad Lib): "Yeah, Red Rider, this is the Cottonmouth in the Psychobilly Cadillac, com'on? This
is the Cotton-mouth, a negatory on the cost of this mo-chine, there, Red Rider, you might
say I went right up to the factory and picked it up, it's cheaper that way. What model is
it?. . . . .Well, it's a 49, 50, 51, 52, 53, 54, 55, 56. 57. 58. 59 automobile. 60, 61,
62, 63, 64, 65, 66, 67, 68, 69 automobile. . . . .70, 71, 72, 73. . . . .

ONEY

Words and Music by
JERRY CHESNUT

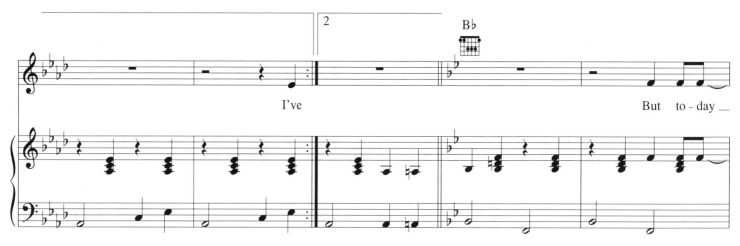

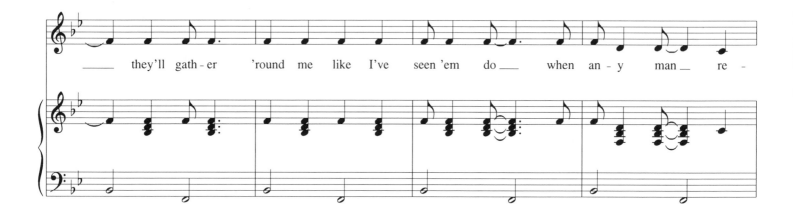

I've ... they'll gath-er 'round me like I've seen 'em do ___ when an-y man re-

tires. Then old

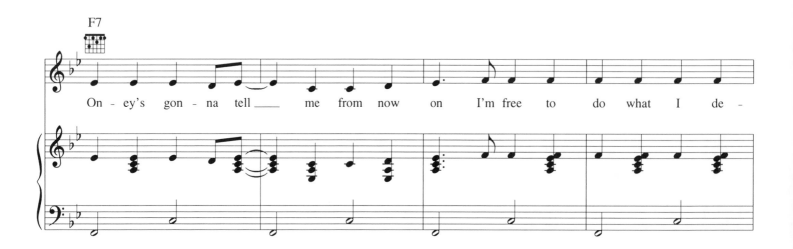

On-ey's gon-na tell ___ me from now on I'm free to do what I de-

sire.   He'll pre - sent me with that

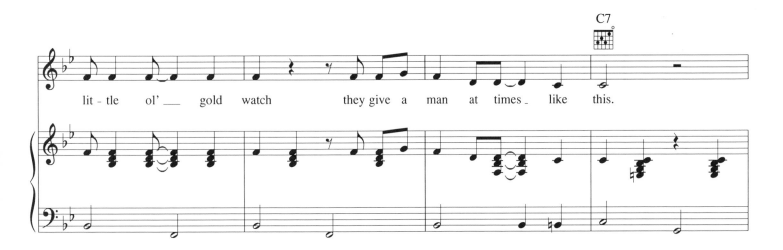

lit - tle ol' __ gold watch   they give a man at times _ like this.

But there's one thing he's not

count-in' on: __ to-day's the day I give ol' On - ey his.

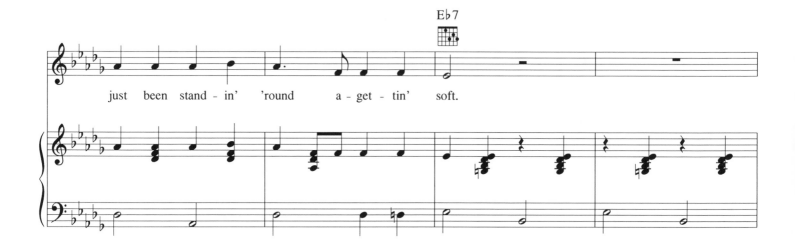

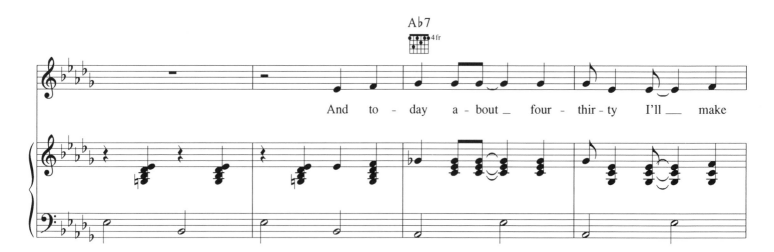

When I'm gone I'll be re-mem-bered as a work-in' man __ that

put his point __ a-cross with a

right hand full of knuck-les, 'cause to-day I show __ ol' On-ey who's the

Repeat and Fade

boss.

Mmm, what time is it? 4:30? Hey, Oney! Oney! Ha ha ha!

ORANGE BLOSSOM SPECIAL

Key of C (C-B)

Words and Music by
ERVIN T. ROUSE

*Chord names and diagrams for guitar.

MCA music publishing

track! _____ — It's the OR - ANGE BLOS - SOM SPE - CIAL _____
shoes. _____ I'll ride that OR - ANGE BLOS - SOM SPE - CIAL _____
line. _____ — It's that OR - ANGE BLOS - SOM SPE - CIAL _____

(Opt. Repeat)

1. C

— — bring - in' my — ba - by back. I'm
— and lose __ these __ New _ York
— — roll - in' down the Sea - board

2. C
To Instrumental Interlude. 3. Fine
C7

blues. line. _____

Instrumental Interlude

Scherzando

F

Bb

mf

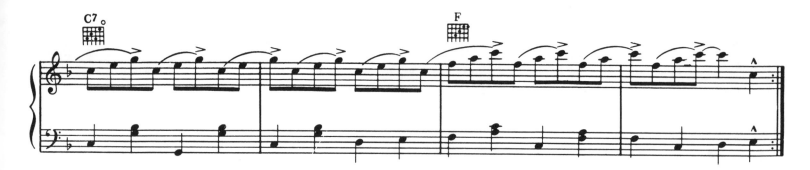

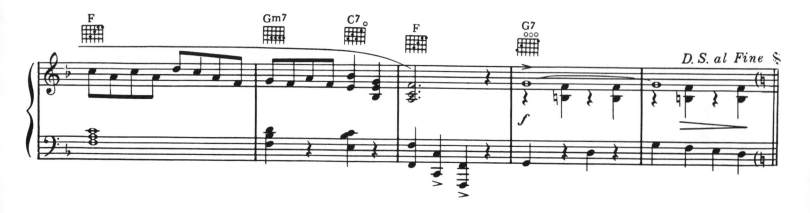

(Ghost)
RIDERS IN THE SKY
(A Cowboy Legend)

from RIDERS IN THE SKY

By STAN JONES

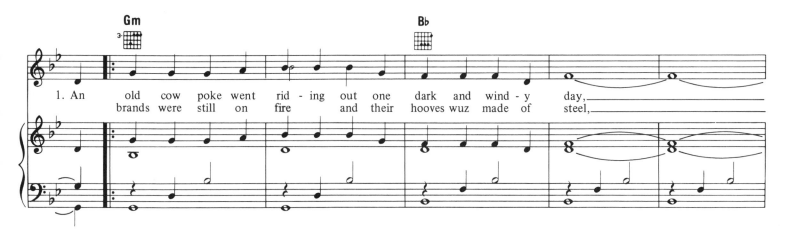

1. An old cow poke went rid-ing out one dark and wind-y day,
brands were still on fire and their hooves wuz made of steel,

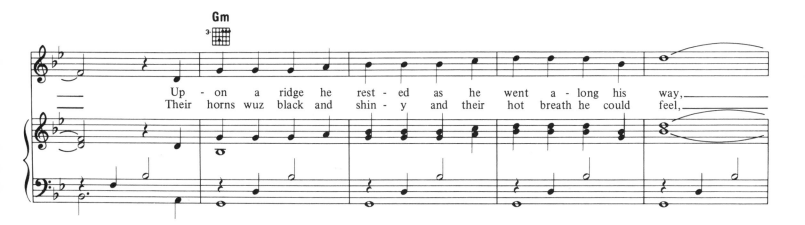

Up-on a ridge he rest-ed as he went a-long his way,
Their horns wuz black and shin-y and their hot breath he could feel,

3. Their faces gaunt their eyes were blurred and shirts all soaked with sweat,
   They're ridin' hard to catch that herd but they ain't caught them yet,
   'Cause they've got to ride forever on that range up in the sky
   On horses snortin' fire As they ride on, hear their cry.
   Yi - pi - yi - ay, Yi - pi - yi - o, The Ghost Riders In The Sky.

4. As the riders loped on by him he heard one call his name,
   "If you want to save your soul from hell a ridin' on our range,
   Then cowboy change your ways today or with us you will ride
   A - try'n to catch the devil's herd Across these endless skies."
   Yi - pi - yi - ay, Yi - pi - yi - o, the ghost herd in the sky. Ghost Riders In The Sky.

THE REBEL - JOHNNY YUMA

Words and Music by RICHARD MARKOWITZ
and ANDREW FENADY

RING OF FIRE

Words and Music by MERLE KILGORE
and JUNE CARTER

Moderately Bright

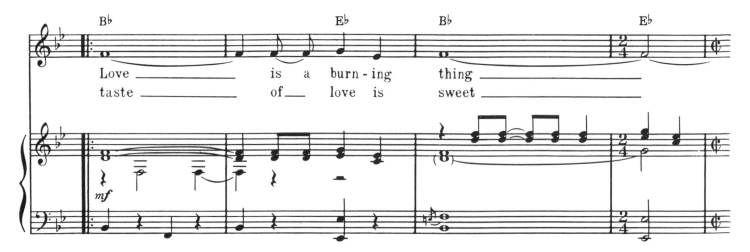

Love _____ is a burn-ing thing _____
taste _____ of_ love is sweet _____

And it makes _____ a fi - ry
When_ hearts _____ like ours _

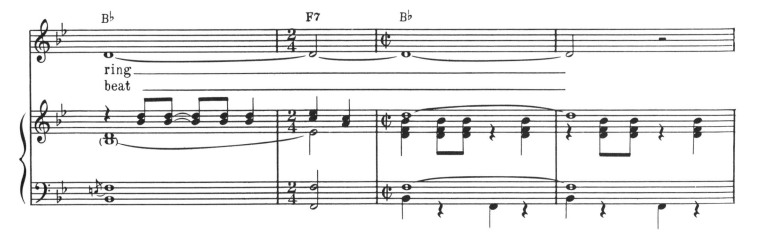

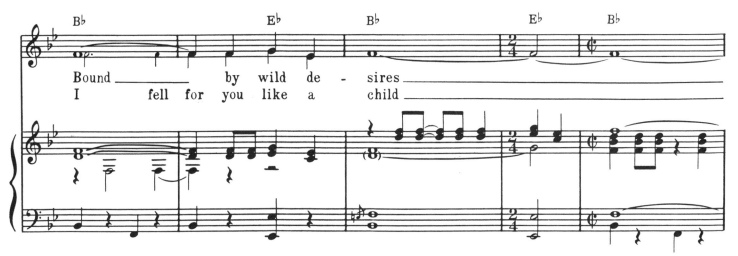

SUNDAY MORNIN' COMIN' DOWN

By KRIS KRISTOFFERSON

SINGIN' IN VIETNAM TALKIN' BLUES
(Bring the Boys Back Home)

Words and Music by
JOHN R. CASH

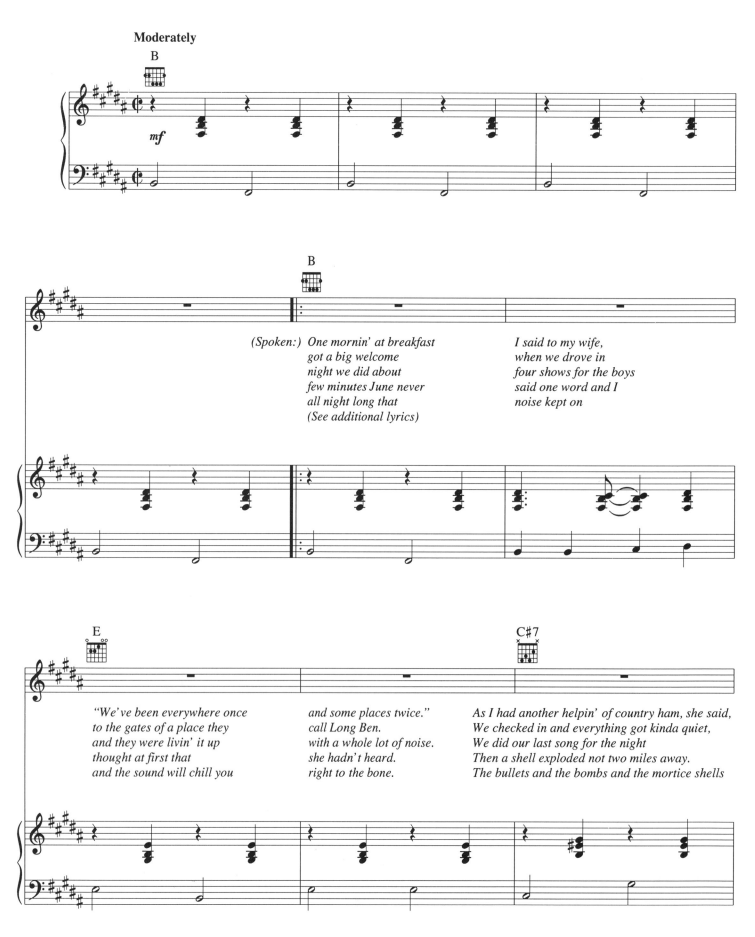

Additional Lyrics

Well, when the sun came up, the noise died down. We got a few minutes sleep and we were sleepin' sound.
Then a soldier knocked on our door and said, "Last night they brought in 7 dead and 14 wounded" and "Would we come down to
the base hospital and see the boys?" Yeah.

So, we went to the hospital ward by day and every night we were singin' away. Then the shells and the bombs till dawn
again and the helicopters brought in the wounded men night after night, day after day, comin' and a-goin'.

So we sadly sang for them our last song and reluctantly we said, "So long." We did our best to let them know that we care for every
last one of them that's over there, whether we belong over there or not. Somebody over here loves 'em and needs 'em.

Well, that's about all that there is to tell about that little trip into living hell. And if I ever go back over there any more, I hope
there's none of our boys there for me to sing for. I hope that war is over with and they all come back home to stay in peace.

SO DOGGONE LONESOME

Words and Music by
JOHN R. CASH

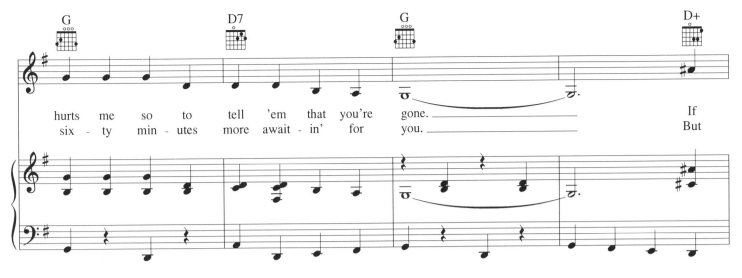

hurts me so to tell 'em that you're gone. _____ If
six - ty min - utes more await - in' for you. _____ But

they ask me, I guess I'd be de - ny - in' _____ 'cause
I guess I'll keep wait - in' till you're with me, _____ 'cause

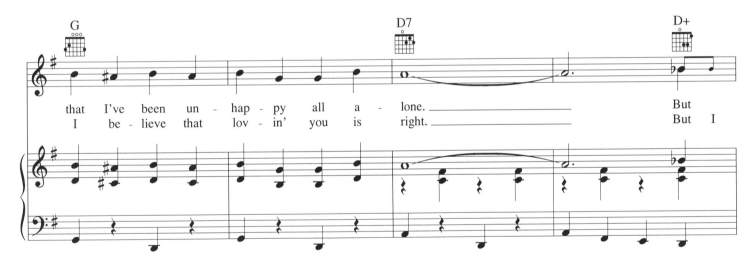

that I've been un - hap - py all a - lone. _____ But
I be - lieve that lov - in' you is right. _____ But I

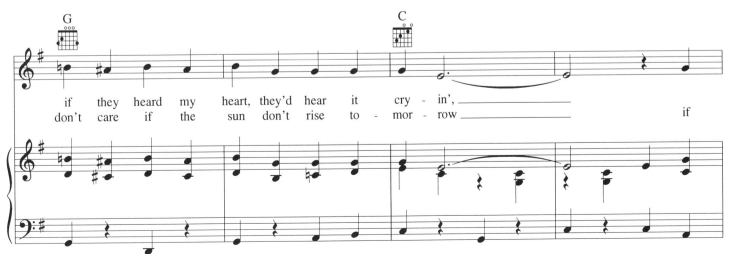

if they heard my heart, they'd hear it cry - in', _____ if
don't care if the sun don't rise to - mor - row _____ if

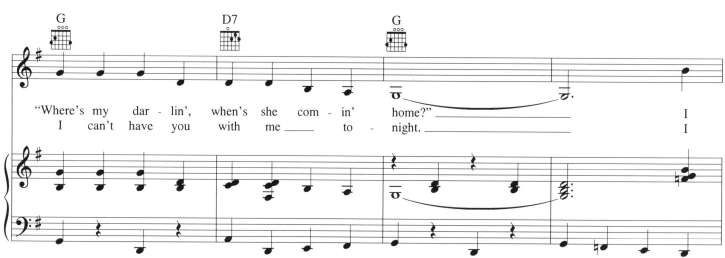

"Where's my dar - lin', when's she com - in' home?" _____ I
I can't have you with me ___ to - night. _____ I

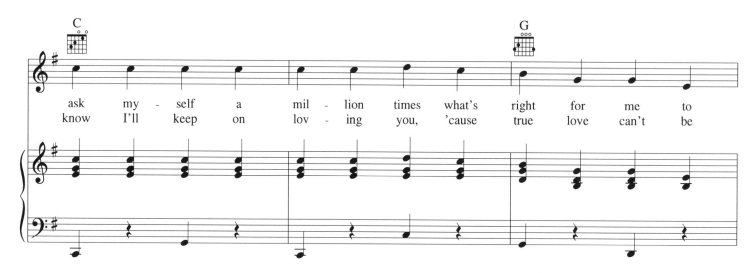

ask my - self a mil - lion times what's right for me to
know I'll keep on lov - ing you, 'cause true love can't be

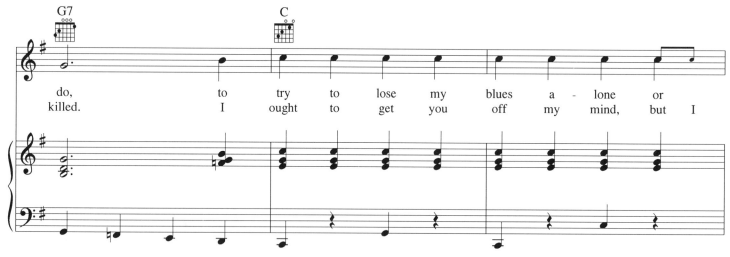

do, to try to lose my blues a - lone or
killed. I ought to get you off my mind, but I

hang a - round with you. But I think it's pret - ty
guess I nev - er will. I could have a doz - en

good un - til that moon comes shin - in' through, and
oth - ers, but I know I'd love you still,

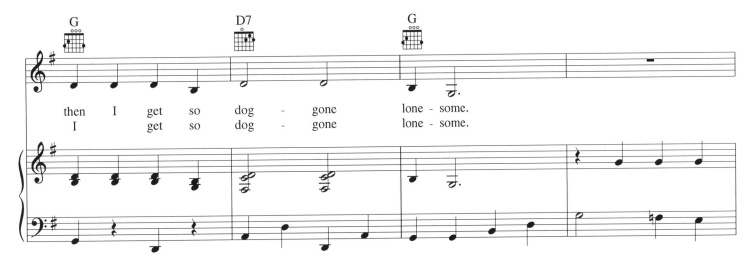

then I get so dog - gone lone - some.
I get so dog - gone lone - some.

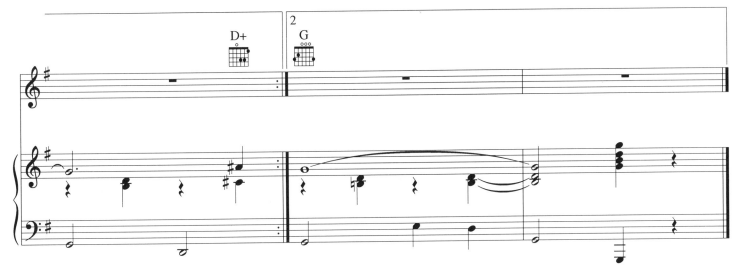

TENNESSEE FLAT TOP BOX

Words and Music by
JOHNNY CASH

Bright Country Two-Beat

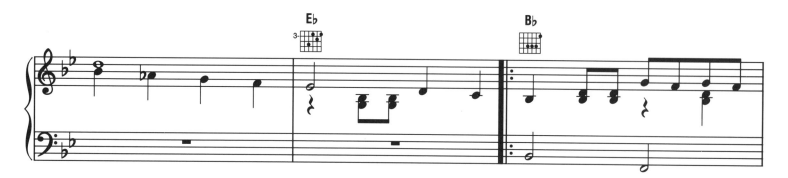

lit - tle cab - a - ret __ in a South Tex - as
could - n't ride or wran - gle and he nev - er cared to
one day he was gone __ and no - one ev - er

In a
Well, he
Then

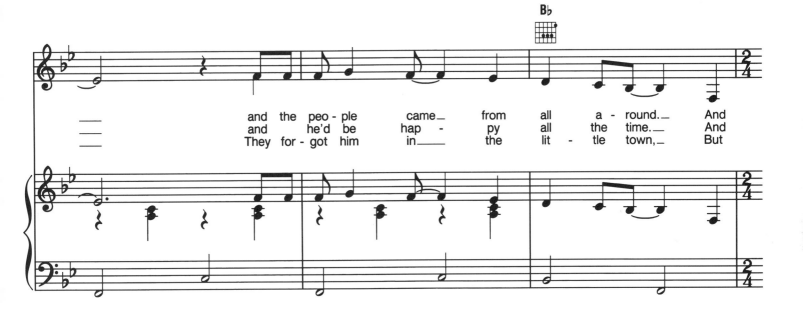

Aus - tin_____ were slip - ping a - way_____ from
nine - ty_____ were snap - ping fin - gers,
bout him_____ and hung a - round_____ the

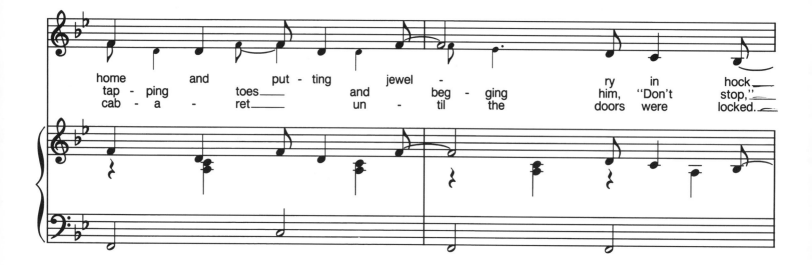

home and put - ting jewel - ry in hock_____
tap - ping toes_____ and un - til beg - ging him, "Don't stop,"_____
cab - a - ret_____ un - til the doors were locked._____

_____ to take_____ a trip_____ to go and
_____ and hyp - no - tized,_____ and fas - ci -
_____ And then one day_____ on the hit pa -

UNDERSTAND YOUR MAN

Words and Music by
JOHNNY R. CASH

Moderately

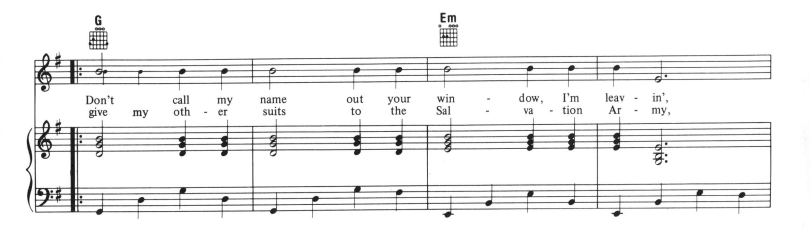

Don't call my name out your win - dow, I'm leav - in',
give my oth - er suits to the Sal - va - tion Ar - my,

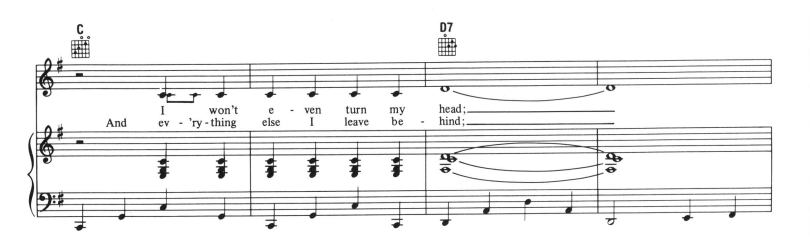

I won't e - ven turn my head;
And ev - 'ry - thing else I leave be - hind;

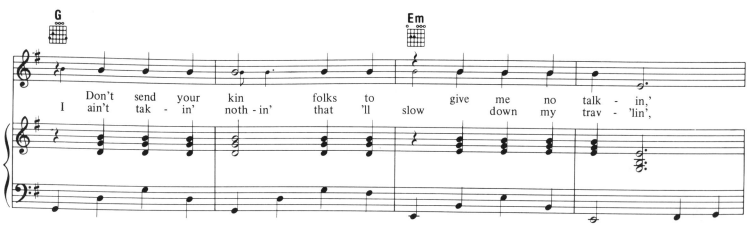

Don't send your kin folks to give me no talk-in,'
I ain't tak-in' noth-in' that 'll slow me down my trav-'lin',

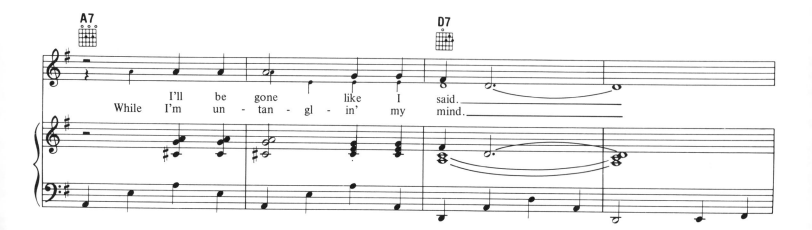

I'll be gone like I said.
While I'm un-tan-gl-in' my mind.

You'd say the same old things that you been say-ing all a-long,
I ain't gon-na re-peat what I said an-y-more,

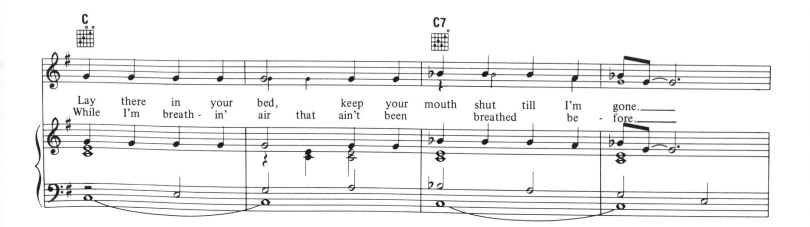

Lay there in your bed, keep your mouth shut till I'm gone.
While I'm breath-in' air that ain't been breathed be-fore.

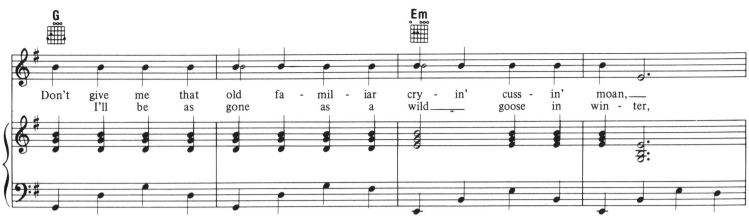

Don't give me that old fa - mil - iar cry - in' cuss - in' moan,___
I'll be as gone as a wild___ goose in win - ter,

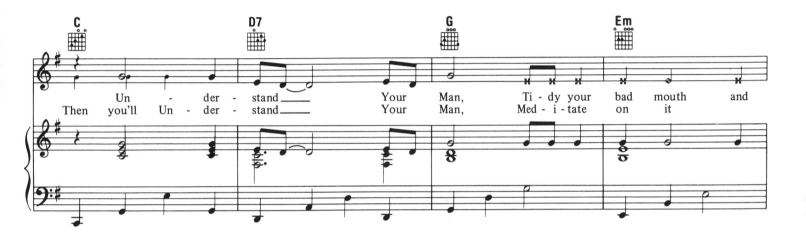

Un - der - stand___ Your Man, Ti - dy your bad mouth and
Then you'll Un - der - stand___ Your Man, Med - i - tate on it

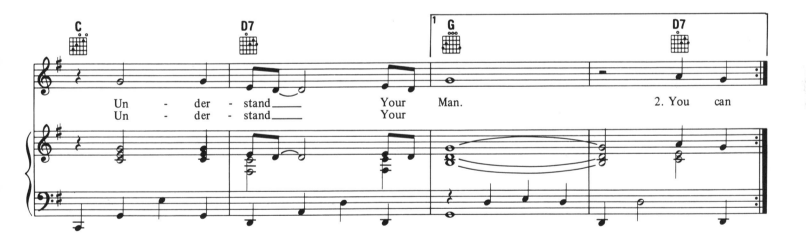

Un - der - stand___ Your Man.
Un - der - stand___ Your

2. You can

Repeat and Fade

Man, You hear me talk - in' hon - ey, Un - der - stand___ Your
Re - mem - ber what I told you,

WHAT IS TRUTH?

Words and Music by
JOHN R. CASH

Moderately

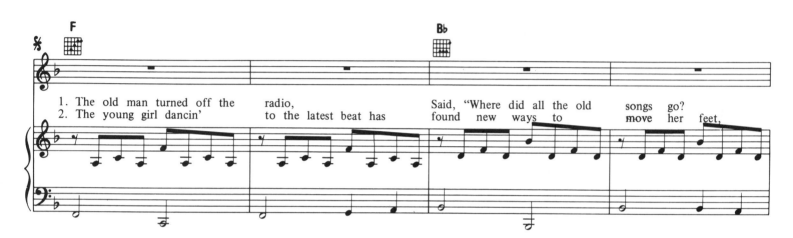

1. The old man turned off the radio, Said, "Where did all the old songs go?
2. The young girl dancin' to the latest beat has found new ways to move her feet,

Kids sure play funny music these days, they play it in the strangest ways."
A young man speaking in the city square, is trying to tell somebody that he cares.

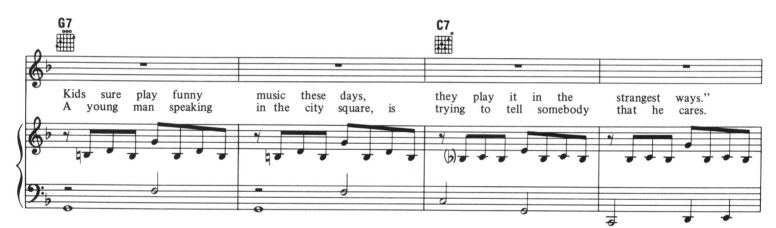

To Coda ⊕

Said, "It looks to me like they've all gone wild, It was peaceful back when I was a child."
Yeah, the ones that you're callin' wild, Are gonna be the leaders in a little while. This

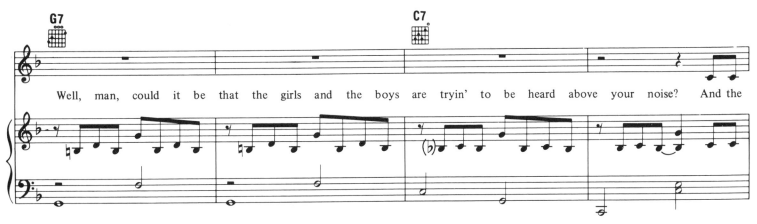

Well, man, could it be that the girls and the boys are tryin' to be heard above your noise? And the

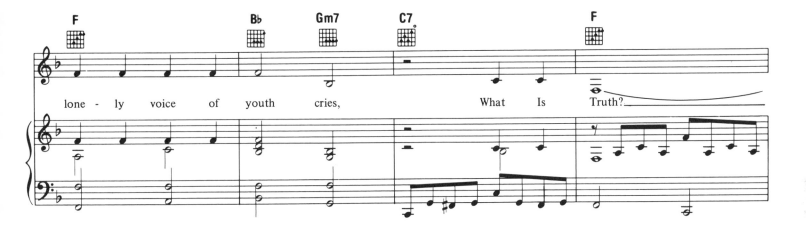

lone - ly voice of youth cries, What Is Truth?___

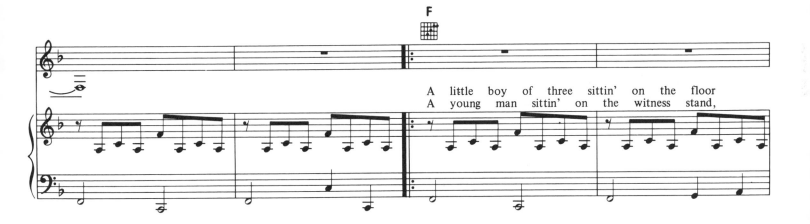

A little boy of three sittin' on the floor
A young man sittin' on the witness stand,

looks up and says, "Daddy, what is war?" "Son, that's when people fight and die."
The man with the book says "Raise your hand." "Repeat after me, I solemnly swear."

WITHOUT LOVE

Written by
NICK LOWE

Moderately

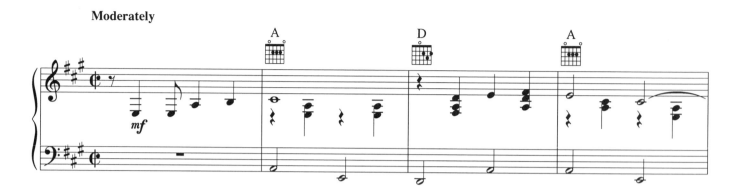

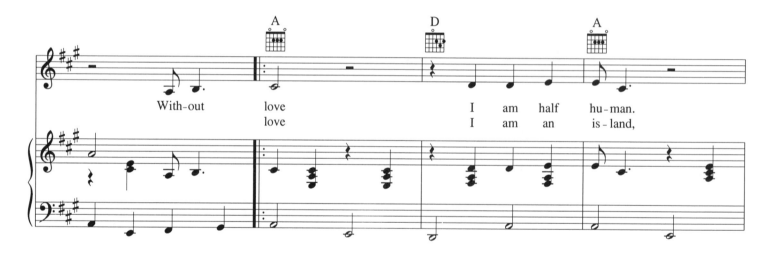

With-out love   I am half hu-man.
love   I am an is-land,

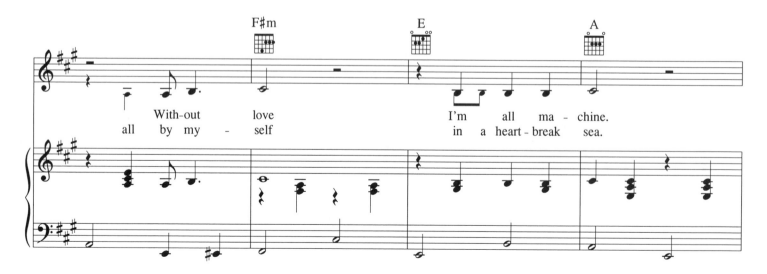

With-out love   I'm all ma-chine.
all by my-self   in a heart-break sea.

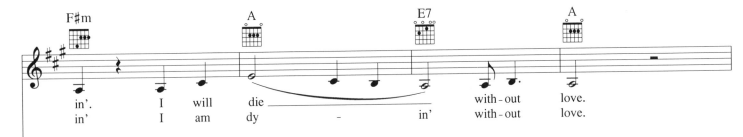

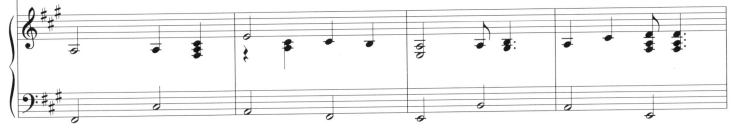

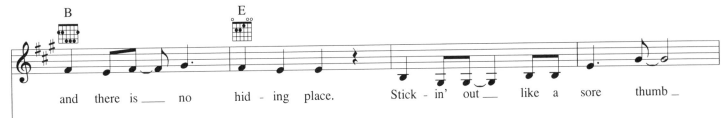

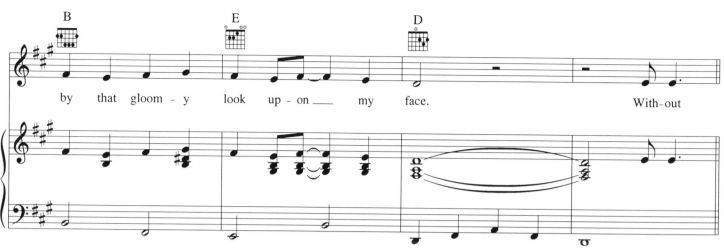

by that gloom-y look up-on ___ my face. With-out

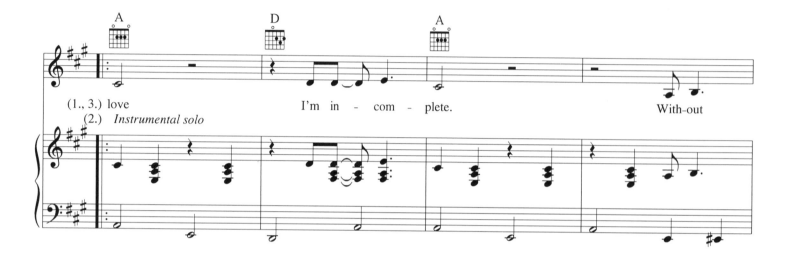

(1., 3.) love I'm in - com - plete. With-out
(2.) *Instrumental solo*

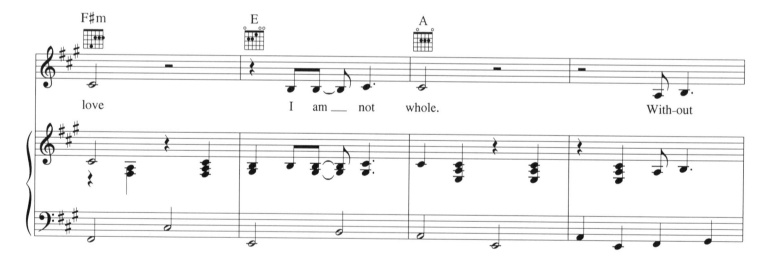

love I am __ not whole. With-out

love I'm bare - ly on my ___ feet. I am

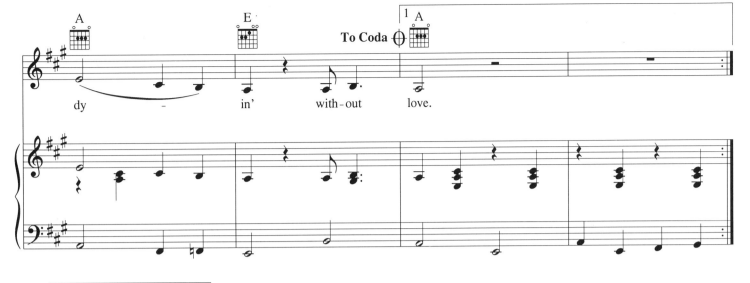

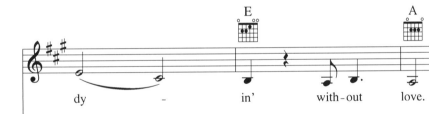

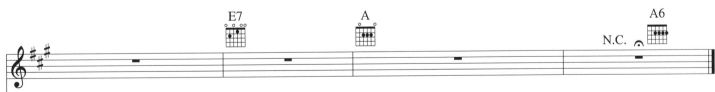

WHAT DO I CARE

Words and Music by
JOHNNY R. CASH

Moderately

VERSE - Freely

When I'm all through, if I have-n't been what they think I should be,

If the to-tal is-n't high e-nough when they fig-ure me,

When I grow old if there's no gray from wor-ry in my